ENTERTAINING AT THE WHITE HOUSE

with *Nancy Reagan*

ENTERTAINING AT THE WHITE HOUSE

with Nancy Reagan

PETER SCHIFANDO *and* J. JONATHAN JOSEPH

DESIGNED BY STEPHEN SCHMIDT

WILLIAM MORROW

An Imprint of HarperCollinsPublishers

FRONTISPIECE: Dinner gathering at White House Rose Garden

PAGE VI: Presidential china from Grover Cleveland Administration

PAGE VIII: Mrs. Reagan, photographed in the Red Room

PAGES X–XI: White House, South Lawn view

PAGE XII: Reagan Presidential scrapbooks

PAGES XIV–XV: In a quiet moment before state dinner festivities begin, Mrs. Reagan looks on as her husband has a word with President and Mrs. Mohammad Zia-ul-Haq of Pakistan. It is customary for the president and first lady to greet the guest of honor to state dinners in the Yellow Room, which is part of the private residence. "It is a beautiful room," recalls Mrs. Reagan. "It is warm and elegant and has a way of making guests feel at home."

HarperCollins books may be purchased for educational, business, or sales promotional use. For information please write: Special Markets Department, HarperCollins Publishers, 10 East 53rd Street, New York, NY 10022.

FIRST EDITION

Designed by Stephen Schmidt / DUUPLEX

Library of Congress Cataloging-in-Publication Data

Schifando, Peter.
    Entertaining at the White House with Nancy Reagan / Peter Schifando and
    J. Jonathan Joseph.—1st ed.
          p. cm.
    Includes bibliographical references.
    ISBN: 978-0-06-135012-2 (hardcover)
    ISBN-10: 0-06-135012-5 (hardcover)
    1. Regan, Nancy, 1923– —Anecdotes. 2. Reagan, Ronald—Anecdotes.
3. Entertaining—Washington (D.C.)—History—Anecdotes. 4. Entertaining—
Washington (D.C.)—History—Pictorial works. 5. White House (Washington,
D.C.)—History—Anecdotes. 6. Washington (D.C.)—Social life and customs—
Anecdotes. 7. Political culture—United States—History—Anecdotes. 8. Presidents'
spouses—United States—Biography—Anecdotes. 9. Presidents—United States—
Biography—Anecdotes. 10. Presidents—United States—Social life and customs—
Anecdotes. I. Joseph, J. Jonathan. II. Title.
    E878.R43S35 2007
    973.927092—dc22
    [B]
                           2007025207

07 08 09 10 11 ID/BT 10 9 8 7 6 5 4 3 2 1

The President and Mrs. Reagan

request the pleasure of your company

Contents

FOREWORD IX

INTRODUCTION XIII

Chapter One

1801: THE HISTORY OF ENTERTAINING 1

Chapter Two

ETIQUETTE AND PROTOCOL 41

Chapter Three

ELEMENTS OF STYLE 71

Chapter Four

PRIVATE GATHERINGS 103

Chapter Five

CELEBRATIONS 129

Chapter Six

MATTERS OF STATE 163

WHITE HOUSE STATE DINNERS 198

EPILOGUE 219

ACKNOWLEDGMENTS 220

NOTES 221

SELECTED BIBLIOGRAPHY 222

Foreword

WHEN MY HUSBAND AND I LEFT WASHINGTON D.C. in 1989, the staff at the White House was kind enough to put together sixteen large scrapbooks commemorating our years there. Many photographs, invitations, and newspaper clippings record the hundreds of luncheons, dinners, and gatherings we hosted during our eight years as president and first lady.

Over the course of many days in the spring of 2006, I met with Peter Schifando and Jonathan Joseph at my home in Los Angeles. We sat around a table that had once been upstairs at the White House. Over iced tea and homemade chocolate chip cookies, we looked through the scrapbooks and I remembered many happy times.

There were parties in the Rose Garden on warm evenings. There was candlelight, and violinists who would stroll among our guests. There were dear friends. Sometimes I would have no recollection of a certain event. In other instances, I would see a photograph from a state dinner or a private gathering and remember the smallest details—the kinds of flowers, a piece of conversation, or a good dessert. Most of all, I remembered dancing with my husband.

Presidents are rarely judged by how well they give a party. Welcoming guests to the White House is, however, an important duty for any administration. State dinners provide foreign guests a window into the United States. The dinners help strengthen bonds between nations and build friendships and goodwill among leaders who might not always see eye to eye.

Entertaining also brought a measure of balance to our lives. No matter how hard the day had been (and we had our share of hard days), my husband and I would often look forward to a fine meal and the company of good friends. I believe that all presidents feel isolated at one time or another. So if you can't go out into the world as much as you'd like, it's important to bring the world to you. When I had to leave Ronnie for a trip away from the White House, I'd make sure to arrange small dinner parties for him with a few close friends. Entertaining was good for the presidency, and good for my husband.

The White House is, first and foremost, a home. Sometimes it's easy to forget this because it is so strongly associated with the power of the presidency. The elegance of the East Room and State Dining Room can overwhelm even heads of industry and royalty. Many guests are too intimidated to put their glasses down on the tables, or to sit on the sofas in the Red Room. Yet we tried to have our guests feel that they were being welcomed into a residence, not an institution.

There are few rules to guide a novice first lady. She can decide for herself which causes she wishes to support. Whether she likes it or not, as the president's wife, she is automatically considered the premier hostess in the country. Ronnie and I did have some prior experience at formal entertaining, first from our years in Los Angeles and then in the governor's office in California. Still, nothing can prepare one for the elegance and scale of White House entertaining.

My first visit to the White House was in 1967 for a dinner hosted for the country's governors. I remember feeling a tremendous sense of history and elegance. When my husband became president in 1981, I wanted our guests to feel that very same sense that I did when they entered the White House for the first time. We knew that for many of our guests, the night would be one of the most memorable in their lives. We wanted to get it right every time.

Luckily for me, after nearly 200 years, the White House staff had refined entertainment to an art form. They had been through just about everything (including wars, deaths, and scandals large and small), so there was little that ruffled them. They were remarkable in both their skill and their loyalty, not just to the sitting president, but also to the house itself. Ronnie and I paid them the respect of assuming they would get the job done. They did, beautifully, over and over again.

We were also helped by talented and capable friends who shared our commitment to making the White House the best it could be.

There are many stories about those wonderful days in the White House. This is our book on the beauty and history of entertaining at the President's House.

NANCY REAGAN
Los Angeles, 2007

Introduction

"THE FIRST LADY IS COMING TO SEE US NEXT WEEK," announced Ted Graber, the interior designer whom Nancy Reagan chose to help with the redecoration of the White House. When I started working with Ted, his commitment to this task was clearly his most important duty. Often, he left Los Angeles on short notice to go to Washington. Although consulting with Mrs. Reagan and her staff on projects was top priority, the reality of his closeness to the president and first lady seemed removed from the daily life of our design office. Until, that is, Mrs. Reagan came to see Ted in Los Angeles.

Refurbishing and decorating the White House was the crowning achievement of Ted's career. As associate to designer William Haines since 1945, he had seen Los Angeles grow in giant steps. Their design work spanned everything from Hollywood mansions to the American Embassy in London. At the office, in a drawer marked "White House," piles of his drawings, samples, and records lay stacked. When Ted would leave on his sudden trips to Washington, I would open this drawer and look through them. It seemed to me that only an impossible circumstance of events could lead an interior designer to work for a president of the United States.

Once, when I asked Ted what it was like to work for the Reagans, he looked at me crossly and said that he worked at "The People's House." I never forgot it. Ted felt an obligation to do his best work at The People's House for the American people. It was a very special honor for him.

Our office phone often rang with calls from the White House. Rex Scouten, the White House's chief usher, and Ted had become close friends. Their mutual respect and admiration made it much easier to accomplish projects between coasts. They had frequent conversations about the progress of events in planning, menus, color schemes, and sometimes politics, and Ted enjoyed them immensely. When Mrs. Reagan called directly, I listened to him laugh and tell jokes, always ending with a kind word and sympathetic expression related to the stresses and events of the day.

Ted had great respect for Ronald Reagan. He always recalled the president's warmth and humor, his easy and friendly manner.

He also enjoyed working with Mrs. Reagan on the private quarters; he never had problems making choices or decisions, as her ideas were always clear and practical. He was thrilled to have access to the vast inventory of unused and forgotten furniture stored in government warehouses. These American antiques proved a treasure trove for use in the White House. Restoring broken and forgotten chests, tables, and chairs became a full-on task for the White House cabinet shop. Ted found this work deeply gratifying and received numerous compliments for his efforts.

He took great pride in helping to determine how the country would be represented to the nations of the world through White House entertaining. He had boundless praise for the tremendous efforts and seamless coordination of the White House staff. A staggering fifty-five state dinners and numerous private events were held at the White House during the Reagan years. The tremendous importance of those events to our country and the good will they fostered between nations is now honored in history.

On the day of Mrs. Reagan's visit to Ted's office in 1988, Secret Service guarded the street and stood on watch surrounding the building. The visit was scheduled to discuss the remodeling and design of another project, the Reagans' future home in Los Angeles. Ted arranged for a small lunch to be served on the office conference table. He asked me to gather flowers to fill vases for the occasion. Linen and silver were laid out and food was carefully presented on beautifully arranged plates. A silver tray of homemade cookies was presented for dessert. After lunch, he presented the decoration scheme of the new house with colored drawings showing how all of the Reagan furniture from the White House would be used and have a prominent place. "It looks just fine," Mrs. Reagan said with a smile and a friendly laugh among friends. It felt as if I was seeing history happen right in front of me. In less than an hour, an aide knocked at the door; it was time for the first lady to go.

Years before, during the first Reagan administration, Jonathan Joseph and I were riding in a taxicab on Park Avenue in New York City. At one point, the traffic stopped and we glanced at the limousine next to us heading south. In the back seat, alone, was

Mrs. Reagan. Impulsively Jonathan waved to her. She looked at us, smiled, and waived back. It never crossed our minds that one day we would be working with the first lady. Jonathan and I worked together as interior designers in Boston for sixteen years before relocating to Los Angeles. We have been fortunate to have had opportunity to work closely with the Reagans on the Ronald Reagan Presidential Library in Simi Valley, as well as on the decoration of their residence in Los Angeles.

A large box of photographs kept by Ted Graber sparked the idea for this book. In it, neatly arranged by event, were menus, invitations, schedules, and copies of official White House photographs taken on his visits to Washington. The photographs were records of table arrangements, flower displays, dessert presentations, Christmas decorations, and holiday preparations. These were reminders of what choices had been made, what had been successful, and what might be used again for the many occasions and dinners that needed to be coordinated with Mrs. Reagan when they planned events together. There were also candid shots showing the fun of working at the President's House and the camaraderie Ted enjoyed with the White House staff.

In setting up President Reagan's offices in Century City in Los Angeles, we custom-designed a pair of special bookcases to hold a set of enormous scrapbooks prepared by the White House staff. Thousands of newspaper clippings, magazine articles, photographs, and memorabilia were chronologically arranged in thirty volumes. The bookcases were placed on prominent display directly outside the president's door. For the many visitors who came to greet him, the scrapbooks were an instant reminder of the hundreds of historical moments and events that spanned his eight years in office.

When their furnishings arrived at the new house in California, another set of scrapbooks prepared for Mrs. Reagan by her White House staff was unpacked and stacked in a closet for safekeeping. In the following years, as her husband's health declined, there were few occasions when it would have been appropriate to ask to see them.

When the time came for us to open the former first lady's scrapbooks, vivid memories of eight years of world events came back to life. It was a deeply moving experience. We are very pleased to share this record of some of those historical events and happy memories.

PETER SCHIFANDO AND J. JONATHAN JOSEPH
Los Angeles, 2007

CHAPTER ONE

1801: The History of Entertaining

1801: The History of Entertaining

IT WOULD BE FITTING TO REPORT THAT THE FIRST public party at the White House was a splendid affair with wine, music, and merriment. History suggests otherwise. As grand and inviting as the new mansion may have been, President John Adams, besieged by ill health and a recent electoral loss to Thomas Jefferson, was probably in no mood for a party.

On January 1, 1801, President and Mrs. Adams stood solemnly in the oval parlor upstairs as they received guests into the partially furnished house. Just a few weeks earlier, workmen's sheds had dotted the surrounding grounds, and the fireplaces were kept burning night and day to dry the plaster. Only half the rooms were complete. The president wore a black velvet suit and bowed formally to each guest. There were, Adams lamented, "few people in this world with whom I can converse. I can treat all with decency and civility . . . but I am never happy in their company."

The President's House, however, was built with entertaining in mind. Even in its unfinished form, the first guests to the new mansion could look out the windows to a sweeping vista of the Potomac River and to the marshes and forests beyond. A large room on the side of the house, later dubbed the East Room, was designed specifically for entertainment and receptions. The house was, in the words of Abigail Adams, "built for the ages."

Architect James Hoban worked along with President Washington to design a mansion that evoked power and legitimacy, but not entitlement and monarchy. It had to be grand enough to impress European courts but also embody our emerging democratic ideals. Then, as now, newcomers to the mansion were often surprised to find themselves in a genteel southern mansion. Although the President's House was the largest private home in America at that time, it retained an intimacy that only heightened the sense of privilege bestowed upon its guests.

The President's House (it would not officially be called the White House for another hundred years) quickly became the center of a new American society. Those who sought favor or jobs could attend a public reception or receive a dinner invitation and court favor with the president or another high official. Equally important, the mansion became a gathering place for the country's finest artists, scientists, and writers. Historically, the house has been a vital crossroads where powerful new ideas could be exchanged.

Presidential entertaining became important to the play of power in the nation's capital. The way a president entertained said a great deal about his presidency. A lively reception or a carefully planned state dinner could build friendships and bestow an aura of competence and legitimacy to an administration.

Presidents have met with scorn for either an excess or lack of White House gatherings. Some, like James Madison, Franklin Roosevelt, and Ronald Reagan, found enormous enjoyment and benefit from a good party. Others entertained at a bare minimum out of a sense of obligation, or for reasons of war or turmoil. Most presidents have understood, however, that to avoid isolation in the rarified atmosphere of the White House, entertaining is indispensable. As Abraham Lincoln observed, leaders "moving only in an official circle are apt to become merely official."

"KING" GEORGE

John Adams, who had been the country's first vice president, adhered closely to a model of entertainment established by George Washington. The first president, who died a year before the mansion was ready for occupants, did not embrace the populist notion that a new form of government would require a new way of greeting guests.

"Washington was dealing with very basic questions about how to govern," observes columnist and historian George Will. "Should he be referred to as 'King George'? Does he make small talk? Should a president shake a guest's hand?"

Washington chose formality. Standing with his back to the fireplace in his Mt. Vernon home, the president kept his hand on his dress sword while the other held his feathered hat. With both hands occupied, a polite bow would mark the introduction. After guests had been received, Washington and his wife would mingle among the crowd. Familiarity was frowned upon; Washington once froze in horror when a well-meaning citizen slapped him on the back as if he were a tavern keeper. Some early parties with Washington were so stifled by European etiquette that, so the story goes, not a single word was spoken. "And those were long dinners," observes Will.

Washington understood, however, that in a new egalitarian system, every American must have access to his leader. He began the custom of receiving callers on New Year's Day, a tradition that continued well into the twentieth century. He also designated certain days and times for casual drop-ins. Yet he could not abide an open-door policy that distracted him from the arduous task of creating a new country. "I could not get relieved from the ceremony of one visit before I had to attend to another," he wrote.

On May 1, 1789, a policy toward the president's entertainment duties was announced in the *Gazette of the United*

ABOVE: The first invitation to a White House reception was delivered by messenger. Abigail Adams filled out many of the invitations herself.

PAGE XVI: Most presidents have understood that entertaining is vital in order to avoid isolation in the White House. President and Mrs. Lincoln, like their predecessors, held frequent receptions in the White House, even during the darkest days of the Civil War. Here, artist Peter F. Rothermel depicts an East Room reception in *The Republican Court in the Days of Lincoln*.

PAGE 2: Howard Taft, then the secretary of war under President Theodore Roosevelt, speaks to guests at a party on the South Lawn in 1905. The outdoor areas of the President's House have been used for entertaining since its earliest days.

States: "We are informed that the President has assigned every Tuesday and Friday between the hours of 2 and 3 for receiving visits; that visits of compliment on other days and particularly Sunday, will not be agreeable to him. It seems to be a prevailing opinion that so much of the President's time will be engaged by various and important business imposed on him by the Constitution that he will find himself constrained to omit returning visits, or accepting invitations to entertainments."

The president would join in the festivities, but not to the detriment of his Constitutional duties.

MR. JEFFERSON'S ROUND TABLE

The third president came into office intent upon showing the European courts that the United States had broken free from its past, both politically and culturally. Thomas Jefferson felt that the austere social protocol of Washington and Adams was wrong for a country that had extricated itself from a monarchy.

To the dismay of high society, Mr. Jefferson (as he preferred to be called) did away with weekly receptions, or by the French term, levees, that had become a mainstay of upscale Washington City. The average American felt more welcome than ever because strangers could simply drop by the President's House and be cordially greeted by its occupant. Unlike his predecessors, Jefferson shook the hands of his guests, thereby setting a precedent that would bedevil presidents from that day foreword. "Mr. Jefferson mingled . . . with all the citizens," one visitor observed.

It was rare to find Jefferson dining alone. In what is now the Green Room, his use of a round table for small parties became a potent symbol for a new democracy; everyone had an equal voice at the president's table. It was also true that there was little chance for quiet gossip away from the ears of the inquisitive host. Jefferson could hear every word of conversation at the small round table. He kept copious notes of each guest and the ideas proffered. Long before press conferences, such gatherings were powerful methods of both obtaining and conveying news and ideas. If a discussion from the dinner reached a newspaper or the halls of the Capitol, the president was able to pinpoint its source.

Although Jefferson believed in government that was "rigorously frugal and simple," his style of entertainment was quite the opposite. Dinner began at four in the afternoon. While the president's table rarely had more than twelve guests, each one enjoyed his own portable serving table from which he could serve himself without interrupting the flow of lofty conversation.

JOHN AND ABIGAIL ADAMS

The first occupants saw both peril and potential in the new President's House. Still sparsely furnished, much remained to be done. Washington City, for all its natural beauty, was considered a swampy backwater lacking in creature comforts. President John Adams, beset by ill health, personal tragedy, and a recent political loss, was not happy in the new mansion. "Shiver, shiver," wrote Abigail Adams, concerned about the difficulty of warming the largest house in the country through the coming winter. It was, as she noted, "built for ages to come…" with rooms on a "grand and superb scale."

THOMAS JEFFERSON

Thomas Jefferson angered Washington society by doing away with the weekly levees that had become an integral part of the city's social life. The new president preferred small dinner parties in what is now the Green Room of the White House, where lucky guests would sip the finest European wines and discuss the great issues of the day. The new president, who preferred to be called "Mr. Jefferson," opened up the President's House to ordinary citizens on New Year's Day and the Fourth of July. Breaking ranks with the first two presidents, Jefferson shook the hand of each guest.

THE FIRST GREAT HOSTESS

Dolley Madison often startled visitors by offering a pinch of snuff from a carved lava box. "But in her hands," observed a guest, "the snuff-box seems only a gracious implement with which to charm." Famed for her ostrich-feathered turbans, Mrs. Madison's easy, earthy charm made her a White House favorite for half a century. Shown here as a young woman in a portrait by Gilbert Stuart, she was a frequent guest at the President's House both before and after her husband's administration. Her weekly drawing rooms, held in what is now the Blue Room, became the center of high society.

The mansion's garden supplied vegetables through the summer and potatoes and root vegetables for winter guests. A dinner might include a partridge shot by a huntsman or by Jefferson's private secretary, Meriwether Lewis, from a stand of trees near Pennsylvania Avenue. Guests could linger over wines imported from Spain, Portugal, France, and Italy.

Fearing disharmony, President Jefferson would rarely mix the company of Federalists with Republicans on the same evening. Jefferson knew that a good dinner party could be more powerful than a speech before Congress and that the alliances and goodwill created over a glass of claret would serve him well in future days. A European monarch could simply wave his hand and his orders would be followed. In this new form of government, only persuasion and consensus could lead to change and action. Thus began a tradition, which continues today, of using the charms of intimate parties at the White House to influence public affairs on a grand scale.

MRS. MADISON'S CRUSHES
By 1809, under the presidency of James Madison, the population of Washington City was booming. Recently elected congressmen from the new western states began to arrive. These men and their families were not part of the landed colonial aristocracy, nor had they taken part in the revolution against the British. These new frontier legislators would have a great deal of power, and they would need to be entertained. Without a chance to vent political steam, build alliances, meet and greet the people with whom policy is made, the fledgling government could fail.

The first lady responded to this new challenge brilliantly, with a series of weekly receptions that quickly became the focus of Washington City's social whirl. Aware that French terms such as *salon* or *levee* might be off-putting, Dolley Madison preferred the "drawing room." Breaking away from Jefferson's penchant for elitist dinners, Dolley Madison created a setting in which all manner of Americans were welcome and had access to the president, if only for a moment. "Many people . . . made appointments to meet each other there," one guest would later write. "People of musical accomplishments sang and played their best. . . . People of wit made their best jokes."

In contrast to the staid gatherings of Washington and Adams and the small round table dinners of Jefferson, Wednesday night at the Madison White House was a lively affair with as many as four hundred guests clamoring for cook-ies, punch, and Madeira wine in the overflowing public rooms. The parties were so crowded that guests referred to them as "Mrs. Madison's Crushes."

"It was impossible for the servants to get near everyone," observed one guest. "And if they attempted it, the good things (to eat) would all slip away before they succeeded."

This was an expensive proposition for Madison and subsequent presidents. For more than a century the president paid for all staff, food, and entertaining out of his salary. This was fine for landed gentry, but less wealthy presidents, including Lincoln, were staggered by the costs of leadership.

Still, Dolley Madison's receptions set the right tone for a new democracy and offered the powerful message that the government was in good hands. At first, a letter of introduction or a previous meeting with the president was required for admittance, but before long nearly anyone was allowed to attend White House parties. There are stories of cab drivers dropping off fares, tethering the horses, and then doubling back to the President's House for a word with James Madison. As historian Catherine Allgor observes, "Dolley combined sumptuous settings and regal sartorial choices with an inclusiveness that was downright democratic."

Access to power is power. Although Mrs. Madison professed ignorance of such worldly matters, Allgor argues that the first lady knew it was much easier to forge political alliances in the Blue Room than on the floor of the Capitol. At a time of political rancor, enemies could literally put aside their swords for a convivial evening. President Madison could have a personal encounter with every single congressman—no small task either now or in 1813. Mellowed by a glass of wine, a legislator might feel free to suggest an idea that he might otherwise not mention on the floor of Congress.

Mrs. Madison's larger goal was to bolster her husband's presidency, which she did quite effectively. Yet, armed with earthiness and acumen, she never became too regal in her approach. She struck a balance that every subsequent White House administration has sought to achieve.

The first White House hosts forged a new style of entertaining for a new form of government. Yet, after more than two hundred years, the very same challenges and questions faced by Washington, Jefferson, and Madison are relevant to the presidency today. At once a home, an office, and a place of entertainment, the White House is where our country's spirit of history, democracy, and hope shine most brightly.

JOHN QUINCY ADAMS

Although well versed in history and current affairs, John Quincy Adams dreaded his role as host. The frequent receptions had become, in his own words, "more and more insupportable to me." His wife, Louisa, who suffered from migraines and depressions, would often plan dinner parties then fail to attend. One guest observed that anyone seated next to President Adams would have "a hard time of it."

JAMES MONROE

Not all presidents or first ladies had Dolley Madison's gift for putting guests at ease. Some, still clinging to European formality, were stiff as boards. "Not a whisper broke on the ear to interrupt the silence of the place, and every one looked as if the next moment was to be his last!" observed one dinner guest of President James Monroe.

ANDREW JACKSON

"The great wood-fires in every room, the immense number of wax lights softly burning, the stands of camellias.... After going through all this silent waiting fairyland, we were taken to the State Dining Room where there was a gorgeous supper table shaped like a horseshoe, and covered with every good and glittering thing French skill could devise...."
—A guest to the Andrew Jackson White House, 1834

JOHN TYLER

Entertaining has been used to help establish the validity of an administration. Following the death of President William Henry Harrison in 1841, John Tyler became the first vice president to replace an elected president. It was a novel and stressful time in American politics: some labeled Tyler's new position "the accidency." With the help of skilled hostess Dolley Madison, Tyler bolstered his position by increasing the amount of White House entertaining, thereby raising his visibility in Washington society. If he was giving parties at the White House, then he really must be the president after all.

Even before the White House was built, presidents and first ladies have struggled to find a balance between familiarity and formality. Martha Washington was criticized as "too queenly" for often greeting guests while standing on a raised platform. The dynamic continues today, with each administration striving to be both egalitarian and presidential. "It has always been a challenge to have entertaining that represents the loftiness of the office while retaining the friendliness of a family home," observes historian William Seale. This Currier and Ives print from 1876 depicts a reception early in Washington's presidency.

President Grover Cleveland greets guests in the East Room. A witness to Cleveland's receptions recalled that an aide would ask each guest his name and then repeat it for President and Mrs. Cleveland, who would then greet each guest by name and say, "So glad to see you." Before security concerns made such receptions impossible, any American willing to wait in line had a chance to meet the president in his own home. Access to the president, if even for a moment, is a powerful symbol of democracy.

OVERLEAF: The President's House was still lit by candles and Argand lamps when this, the first known photograph of the White House, was taken in 1846. Two years later, the mansion switched to high-tech gaslights. First Lady Sarah Polk did not fully trust the new technology and insisted that the chandeliers in the Blue Room retain their wax candles. Mrs. Polk's intuition was proven right when the gas failed during a nighttime reception, and guests crowded into the Blue Room for illumination.

"I must go to dinner. I wish it were to eat pickled herring, Swiss cheese, and a chop... instead of the French stuff I shall find."

—PRESIDENT GROVER CLEVELAND, writing to a friend before a White House dinner

EDITH WILSON

"My first public appearance as the wife of the president was at a reception to the diplomatic corps. There were 3,328 guests. I wore a white gown brocaded in silver with long white tulle drapery, then known as 'angel sleeves.' It was thrilling, the first time, to greet all the cabinet in the Oval Room upstairs, and then with the president precede them down the long stairway with the naval and military aides forming an escort, the Marine Band playing 'Hail to the Chief,' and the waiting mass of guests as we passed into the Blue Room."

—EDITH WILSON, wife of President Woodrow Wilson

ELEANOR ROOSEVELT

For Sunday luncheons, Eleanor Roosevelt would gather the leading writers, artists, actors, and dancers of the day. The first lady would use a large silver chafing dish brought from the Roosevelt mansion in Hyde Park to prepare eggs so as not to disturb the lofty conversation with clattering plates and servants. In light of the guest list, the staff referred to the menu as "scrambled eggs with brains."

BOOKER T. WASHINGTON

An invitation to the White House can create a furor. A quiet
dinner held by Teddy Roosevelt for educator and author Booker
T. Washington in 1901 angered many in the South. "God set up
the barrier between the races," chastised the *Macon Telegraph*.
"No president of this or any other country can break it down."
Others declared that because of Washington's presence, no
southern woman should accept an invitation to the White House.
Washington, the first African American to dine with a president at
the White House, is shown working in his office around 1910.

one thousand eight hundred and sixty three; and of the Independence of the United States of America the eighty-seventh.

Abraham Lincoln

By the President:

William H. Seward
Secretary of State

ABRAHAM LINCOLN

White House entertaining can take a physical toll on its occupants. On New Year's Day 1863, President Lincoln greeted so many guests at a reception that his hand was, as he recalled, "swollen like a poisoned pup...." But his signature was required later that day. "Now this signature is one that will be closely examined. If they find my hand trembled they will say 'He had some complications; but anyway, it must be done....' I never in my life felt more certain that I was doing right, than I do signing this paper." Undaunted, Lincoln signed the Emancipation Proclamation in a steady, strong cursive.

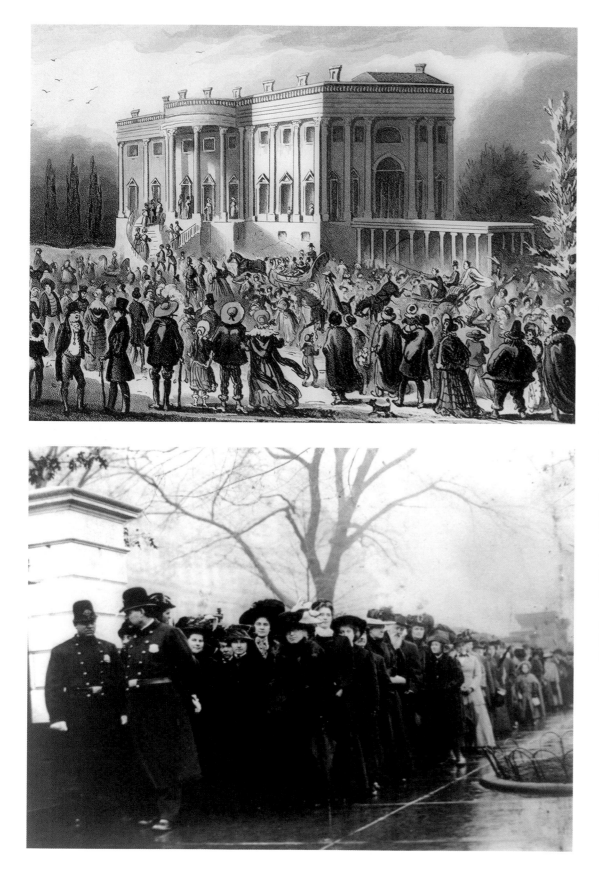

TOP: President Andrew Jackson was perhaps too welcoming to Americans after his 1829 inauguration. Thousands of well-wishers swarmed the President's House for a reception that ended in vandalism, drunkenness, and thievery. "Cut glass and china to the amount of several thousand dollars had been broken in the struggle to get refreshments," wrote one witness. "Ladies fainted, men were seen with bloody noses...." Some revelers, staying on after the party had ended, were found passed out on sofas. This rendering by artist Robert Cruikshank from 1841 is aptly titled *President's Levee, or all Creation going to the White House.*

BOTTOM: The line for a New Year's Day reception at the White House, like this one in 1920, often snaked for blocks. So powerful was the draw of receptions that crowds would wait in line up to fourteen hours on frigid days, only to be turned away. Hundreds would end up disappointed, but would often return the next year to try again. The crowds were so enormous that workers would construct a temporary wooden bridge through a window of the White House to disgorge guests. Local police would peruse the lines for known pickpockets and women of questionable moral judgment.

OPPOSITE: Guests of President Theodore Roosevelt gather on the South Lawn in 1905.

ABOVE: A delegation of Native Americans from the Southern Plains poses in the White House conservatory on March 27, 1863. Despite ongoing tensions with settlers and soldiers, Native Americans were frequent guests to the White House. On one such visit, First Lady Dolley Madison retired to her bedroom to find a guest, in full war paint, standing behind her bedroom door.

OPPOSITE: President Andrew Johnson meets with members of the Yankton, Santee Sioux, and Upper Missouri Sioux tribes in the East Room in 1867.

OVERLEAF: Grazing animals on the South Lawn were lovely to look upon from afar. But on warm summer days guests in the State Dining Room would sometimes get an unwelcome whiff through an open window. Here, a group of sheep in 1919 keep the South Lawn grass trimmed.

ABOVE: The South Lawn of the White House often resembled a park on a Sunday afternoon. Here, guests at a 1906 reception enjoy the grass and a view of the mansion.

LEFT: The crowd celebrates the Fourth of July, 1982. Although security concerns have curtailed the use of the South Lawn for large receptions, it is still used frequently for holiday gatherings.

LEFT: The East Room sits in quiet splendor in 1903. Although its décor has evolved over the decades, the East Room of the White House remains an epicenter of American history. It is here where presidents who have died in office lay in state. Thomas Jefferson turned the south end of the room into an office and bedchamber for his secretary, Meriwether Lewis. Abigail Adams hung her laundry across its elegant expanse. Abraham Lincoln celebrated the ascension of Ulysses S. Grant to general-in-chief of the Union Army. Many of the great musicians of the last two hundred years have performed here.

ABOVE: Cloth enclosures protect the East Room chandeliers from dust while not in use.

Women curtsy to President Franklin Pierce during an inaugural
reception, or "levee," in the East Room in 1854.

Reception at the White House, by William Baxter Closson, 1908

TOP: The Green Room is shown in 1904 during the Theodore Roosevelt administration.

BOTTOM: Victorian furnishings are on display in 1890 in the Green Room.

OPPOSITE: This daguerreotype from around 1860 is one of the earliest known interior photographs of the White House. Located just off the East Room, the Green Room has been a center of White House entertaining since the first days. It was here that Thomas Jefferson held his famous dinner parties and where generations of subsequent guests have had their after-dinner coffee. For decades, musicians and entertainers, from Pablo Casals to Lionel Hampton, have used it as a waiting area before their performances in the East Room.

ABOVE: President Theodore Roosevelt, a dedicated hunter, displayed some of his prize trophies on the walls of the State Dining Room. The animals may have appealed to some guests, but Woodrow Wilson could not eat in their presence and would turn his back on the stuffed heads in order to avert their gaze. President Wilson soon had the prizes removed. They remain in the collection of the Smithsonian.

OPPOSITE: Prepared to see a grand palace, visitors are often surprised to find themselves in a genteel Colonial mansion. But the smaller scale, especially that of the State Dining Room, only heightens the sense of privilege of an invitation to the house. Suggestions to expand the public areas of the White House have been consistently rejected.

TOP: The State Dining Room, 1900

ABOVE: The Blue Room, circa 1900

OPPOSITE: The upstairs living room, now the Yellow Room, 1890

President Andrew Jackson nearly caused a riot in 1837 when he allowed throngs into the President's House to sample a 1,400-pound round of cheese given to him two years earlier by New York cheese makers. So important was the event that shops closed early to allow employees a shot at the four-foot-wide cheese. The house was overrun. Some anxious guests climbed in through the windows of the East Room. The cheese was gone in two hours, but its aroma hovered like a ghost for months.

Manners had improved somewhat by the time Ronald Reagan took office. Here, President and Mrs. Reagan celebrate his 70th birthday—his first in the White House—with staff.

"I took a step, those back of me took a step, and then the great procession, several thousand strong…began to move. We were all going, rich and poor, old and young, noted and obscure, black and white, to be the guests of the man who guided the destinies of the country, which in our own minds we were pleased to term 'the greatest country on Earth.'"

—A guest to the White House on New Year's Day, circa 1898

Entertaining at the White House with Nancy Reagan

CHAPTER TWO

Etiquette and Protocol

Etiquette and Protocol

THERE'S NO LAW THAT SAYS A PRESIDENT MUST BE polite to a foreign diplomat. When British Ambassador Anthony Merry presented his diplomatic credentials to President Thomas Jefferson in 1801, Jefferson greeted him brusquely, wearing a dusty coat and bedroom slippers. Although Jefferson never said as much, his manner and appearance were likely intended to send a powerful message that the new United States had irrevocably separated from England. The boorish behavior, Merry concluded, was, "from design and not from ignorance or awkwardness." In part because of Jefferson's snub, Merry would later urge his British masters to pursue the War of 1812. Thus some historians argue that Jefferson's breech of protocol may have prolonged America's first war.

Most presidents try to play by the rules. Protocol is defined as the common language of global diplomacy. It is a code of etiquette that transcends local customs and thus allows diplomats and officials to treat one another with respect and courtesy regardless of cultural differences. President Calvin Coolidge established the Office of the Chief of Protocol in 1928 after an unfortunate mistake in which wartime enemies were seated together at an official dinner. Since then, the office has been responsible for coordinating visits from chiefs of state and heads of government from around the world.

Although the term *protocol* evokes images of flags and motorcades, it is more often applied to prosaic matters such as seating, cuisine, and guest lists. Seemingly small details such as flowers or the choice of wine can send a powerful diplomatic message. In most cases, protocol is based upon common sense and conventional good manners played out on a global stage. "It's all about making your guests feel respected and welcome," says Leonore Annenberg, chief of protocol for the U.S. State Department for the first year of the Reagan administration. "President and Mrs. Reagan were very good at that."

Hierarchy is a key concern of protocol and thus plays an important role in formal White House entertaining. This pecking order is based on a number of factors, including one's position and length of service in the diplomatic corps. The U.S. State Department keeps a log of the date on which a diplomat first presents his or her credentials to the president. This determines, among many other things, where an ambassador will sit during a state dinner. Power does not necessarily equate with status in this complex international queue. One official at the Reagan White House, for example, was miffed when a job promotion gave him more access to the president but dropped him several notches in the order of protocol.

All foreign delegations must be treated as equal. The details of an arrival ceremony for a state visit from Ghana should be the same as for the president of France. A guest of honor must always arrive last and leave first. He or she is always accorded the seat of honor to the right of either the president or first lady. The State Department makes a special effort to provide delegations from antagonistic countries (such as Israel and Arab states) with precisely the same services. This applies not only to the number of secret service agents and hotel rooms paid for by the State Department, but also to entertainment, flowers, and food. Any perceived slight could have repercussions around the negotiating table. "President Reagan once told me that form and substance are different sides of the same coin," recalls Selwa Roosevelt, the State Department's chief of protocol from 1982 to 1989. "He meant that how you treat people personally is as important as policy."

Although common sense usually wins the day, the myriad rules and subtleties of international protocol can befuddle even the most experienced State Department staffer. In one colorful instance, a delegation from Oman insisted on wearing their ceremonial daggers into the White House for their 1983 state visit. The Secret Service was not pleased about the presence of weapons near President Reagan, who had already survived one assassination attempt. Gahl Hodges Burt, who then worked with the State Department, asked the Secret Service to allow the foreign delegation to wear their decorative daggers. In another instance, an Italian foreign minister was so disturbed by his distance from the president at a state dinner that he threatened to storm out. "You can't believe how upset people can get if they feel they've been slighted," recalls Selwa Roosevelt. "Consistency is vital."

Most delegations will inform the protocol office of any special requirements. One memo that circulated through the White House in 1981 informed staffers that, "Mrs. (Margaret) Thatcher does not like tomatoes, drinks whiskey and soda, and does not smoke." Her husband Dennis, meanwhile, "Does not like rare roast beef and drinks very dry martinis, sometimes without vermouth."

Martinis aside, there are other obvious cultural sensitivities that must also be observed. Neither Arab nor Israeli delegations should be served pork. Indians should not be served beef. Many cultures shun alcohol. Although this sounds straightforward, it is easy to slip. A spinach salad with bacon bits would be considered an affront to an observant Jew, as would a piece of chicken cooked in wine for a Muslim dignitary. In Brazil it is considered rude to offer a single dessert, so the White House would offer more than one. Mexican delegations do not care much for Tex-Mex cooking, which they consider a pale imitation of their own cuisine. While it is acceptable to serve lamb to an Arab delegation, it is also strikingly obvious. Selwa Roosevelt recalls that it was difficult to convince some foreign guests that sparkling cider is nonalcoholic.

White House florists are well versed in protocol as well. Before any state visit, the florist's office will check with the State Department to note any special concerns. Allergies to certain flowers are common, for example. In Japan, white is associated with death. In Italy, chrysanthemums are funereal. In 1985, the protocol office sent notice to the White House that under no circumstance should blue be used during the state visit of President and Mrs. Jayewardene of Sri Lanka, because blue was the color of a violent opposition group in their country. The State Department feared that blue tablecloths or flowers would not only be a personal affront, but that a photo from the visit could be used as a propaganda tool by the opposition.

After decades of experience in dealing with such matters, the State Department and the White House rarely blunder. Issues for which there is little precedent, however, cannot always be anticipated. In 1982, a Moroccan entourage caused a stir by bringing their own portable stoves into the White House to prepare mint tea for King Hassan II and Mrs. Reagan. "The curator was not so happy when they set up their stoves on the antique carpet," recalls Mrs. Reagan. "But the tea was delicious."

TOP AND OPPOSITE: President and Mrs. Reagan greet President Luis Herrera Campins of Venezuela at the North Portico in 1981. *Top:* Chief of Protocol Leonore Annenberg, who had met President Herrera at Andrews Air Force Base, makes introductions. *Opposite:* President and Mrs. Reagan escort the Venezuelan president into the White House.

ABOVE: President and Mrs. Reagan pose with King Hussein and Queen Noor of Jordan before the start of a 1981 state dinner.

PAGE 40: President and Mrs. Reagan pose with President and Mrs. Figueiredo of Brazil before the start of a 1982 state dinner.

PAGE 42: Trumpets herald the arrival of President François Mitterrand of France in 1984.

President and Mrs. Reagan prepare to escort King Hussein and Queen Noor of Jordan down the Grand Staircase and into the East Room for a state dinner in their honor. Protocol dictates that the president, first lady, and their guests be escorted from the room by a Color Guard representing various branches of the military. Before the group makes its way out of the room, the head of the Color Guard asks for "permission to secure the colors," meaning that the flags of the United States and the country of the visiting leader will be wrapped around their flagpoles, indicating that the group is ready to depart. The president responds "Permission granted," and the group makes its way down the stairs.

The Reagans walk toward the State Dining Room with King and
Queen Birendra of Nepal in 1983.

ABOVE: President and Mrs. Reagan escort President Alessandro Pertini of Italy into the East Room in 1982. In a longstanding tradition, the Marine Band plays "Hail to the Chief" as the president enters. In a sign of respect that touched the Reagans, Pertini kissed the American flag during his arrival at the White House. "What a dear man," Mrs. Reagan recalls of the Italian leader.

RIGHT: President and Mrs. Reagan escort Prime Minister Thatcher and her husband, Dennis, down the Grand Staircase in 1981. It was the first of fifty-five state dinners during the Reagan administration.

THE UNITED STATES MARINE BAND AT THE "WHITE HOUSE"

CAPTAIN TAYLOR BRANSON, LEADER

EXCLUSIVE MANAGEMENT
W. L. RADCLIFFE
WASHINGTON,
D.C.

THE MARINE BAND

The Marine Band has been an indispensable part of White House
entertaining since the first reception held at the President's House
in 1801, when its eight members performed for guests of John
and Abigail Adams. Its musicians, now numbering up to seventy,
have serenaded everyone from kings to commoners and have
accompanied iconic performers from Frank Sinatra to Isaac Stern.
The group has participated in every presidential inauguration
since Thomas Jefferson took office. During the Civil War,
President Abraham Lincoln became annoyed when crowds outside
the White House demanded a speech during a concert. "I wish
they would just let me sit out there quietly, and enjoy the music,"
Lincoln said.

OVERLEAF: The Marine Band gives a holiday performance at the
White House.

White House Etiquette

Even the best schooled among us can feel overwhelmed by an invitation
to the President's House. Although the president, first lady,
and their staff will do everything possible to make guests feel welcome
and comfortable, there are a few tips that might be beneficial.
Here, with the help of etiquette expert Letitia Baldrige and others,
is a short primer on White House etiquette.

Say "Yes"

Unless there is a death, illness, or marriage in your family, always try to accept an invitation to the White House. Refusals do occur, much to the dismay of White House staff. Some cabinet members become so blasé about invitations that they accept or reject at will. Frequently, guests fail to show up even though they have said they will attend. Even if you're off on an island, Baldrige says, you should come back.

Seek Fashion Advice

Even sophisticates get it wrong at the White House. Those mistakes often end up on the front page of newspaper style sections across the country. Baldrige recommends a direct call to the White House social secretary for advice on what others will be wearing and what you plan to wear. Just consider a recent White House event at which four women, including the first lady, wore the same dress. Ask specific questions and get it right.

Arrive in Style...

Do not attempt to drive your own car. Use a limousine service that knows the routines of White House entertaining, including shortcuts, correct locations to drop off guests, and the best place to call for them after the event.

...and On Time

There is no such thing as "fashionably late" at the White House. This is a terrible lapse of judgment, and rude not only to the president and first lady but to the visiting dignitary. "People who arrive late are clods," observes Baldrige. "We have a whole society of know-nothings." She advises guests to arrive five to ten minutes early in order to move swiftly through security, check your coat, and get up to the main floor as quickly as possible. You will not want to miss a single moment of a grand American tradition.

Turn to Your Left...Turn to Your Right

Talk with equal enthusiasm to the person on your right and left. The person sitting next to you will likely be one of the most prominent people in the country. He or she may also be a close friend of the president or first lady. Never criticize a president or the administration over dinner. Anything you say could get back to officials in the White House. It is unlikely you will return for the duration of the administration.

Do Not Lobby

"It is the kiss of death to push your agenda at a White House social gathering," says Baldrige. "It's looked upon with disgust." It does happen, however, especially with aggressive young congressmen who are uninitiated to the ways of Washington. Baldrige has seen such behavior lead to banishment from the White House. An experienced White House visitor knows that pushing one's agenda should be done in the days or weeks following a dinner, not during the dinner itself.

When in Doubt, Imitate the First Lady

Confronting a gauntlet of flatware or a finger bowl can be daunting. It is advisable to look to others at your table to check manners. John Musante, green grocer and longtime friend of the Reagans, was invited to a state dinner and sat at Mrs. Reagan's table next to actress Jaclyn Smith. Smith was also a newcomer to the White House, and together they decided to simply follow Mrs. Reagan's lead. When the first lady served herself a small portion from a tray, they did the same. When she used a certain fork, they did as well. By the time a Log Cabin cake was served for dessert, however, Smith's attitude changed. "I don't care how much of that cake Mrs. Reagan serves herself," Smith told Musante. "I'm having a *big* slice."

Do Not Ask for More

It is unacceptable to request second helpings at a White House dinner. The meal has been planned for four courses. It is advisable to serve oneself enough from each tray so as not to go hungry, yet not so much as to appear ravenous.

Chat with the President

After dinner, do not hesitate to approach the president and first lady for a brief conversation. You've been invited to their home, and they will be delighted to speak to you. Do not monopolize the president for more than two or three minutes, however. If one of the military or social aides decides you've overstayed your chat, you will be given a polite invitation to another part of the room.

Leave Gracefully

Protocol dictates that guests should remain until the guest of honor has left a state dinner. In most cases, the president and first lady will remain for a short time before departing up the Grand Staircase to the private quarters of the White House. This will be your cue to have a final dance, a last sip of champagne, and exit through the East Corridor.

Smile. Always, always smile...

LEFT: Protocol in the Lincoln White House, shown in this illustration, was much more restrictive than today. Women, for example, were required to wait while men preceded them through the receiving line to meet the president. Guests would be allowed into the State Dining Room in order of diplomatic ranking. After dinner, rising from a table before the president was a serious breech. Even carriages waiting to meet departing guests would queue up according to rank.

BOTTOM: President and Mrs. Theodore Roosevelt greet guests at a White House reception.

OPPOSITE: An elaborate seating chart illustrates the details of an 1877 dinner for Grand Duke Alexis of Prussia during the administration of Rutherford B. Hayes. The seating was determined by diplomatic ranking.

State Dining Room.

Mr. W. C. Hayes.

Colonel Casey.		Admiral Porter
Baron Schilling		Admiral Boutakoff.
Miss MacFarland	Diner du 19 Avril.	The Attorney Genl.
The Post Master Genl.	Consommé printanier à la royale.	Mrs. Casey.
Miss Schurz	Petites bouchées à la Cardinale.	The Secy. of the Treasy.
The Chief Justice	Filets de bass à la Normande.	Mrs. McCrary.
Mrs. Evarts	Filets de boeuf à la Richelieu.	The Secy. of State
Grand Duke Constantine	Pains de volaille à la Impériale.	Lady Thornton
	Cotelettes d'agneau aux petits-pois.	
	Cimbales d'Olives garnies de filets de pigeons.	
Mrs. Hayes.	Cerrines de foies-gras a la Lucullus.	The President.
Grand Duke Alexis	Punch au Kirsch.	Mrs. Shishkin
Mrs. Waite	Faisans piqués garnis de bécasses aux cressons.	Sir Edward Thornton
	Salade de laitue.	
Mr. Shishkin.	Asperges en branches, sauce à la crème.	Mrs. Sherman
	Ramequins de dijon au parmesan.	
Mrs. Key	Crèmes diplomate au marasquin.	The Secy. of War
The Secy. of the Navy.	Gelées d'Oranges garnies de fraises.	Miss Foote
Miss Platt	Dessert.	The Secy. of the Interior
Genl. Sherman	Café.	Mr Koudrine
Capt. Alexeieff.		Mr. Rogers.

Mr. Andrews.

United States Marine Band.

Dinner to
Nobel Prize Winners of the Western Hemisphere
Dinning Room (127)   Total (177)   April 29, 1962.

ABOVE: A group of Nobel Prize winners were celebrated at a 1962 dinner at the Kennedy White House. Although diplomatic ranking held no sway, this starlike chart was prepared before the dinner to insure a memorable night. Guests included poet Robert Frost, writer James Baldwin, and Dr. Robert Oppenheimer. As at most formal dinners, married couples were separated and placed at different tables. "I think this is the most extraordinary collection of talent, of human knowledge, that has ever been gathered together at the White House," observed President Kennedy. "With the possible exception of when Thomas Jefferson dined alone."

OPPOSITE: Cellist Pablo Casals performed for President and Mrs. Kennedy in 1961. He made his first White House appearance in 1904. President Roosevelt instantly charmed him. "He put his arm around my shoulder after the concert," Casals recalled, "and led me around among the guests, introducing me to everyone and talking all the time. I felt that in a sense he personified the American nation, with all his energy, strength and confidence."

The use of a head table for state dinners has largely disappeared. At the state dinner for Emperor Haile Selassie of Ethiopia, President Lyndon Johnson followed old-school protocol by sitting with the wife of the guest of honor to his right. Once the norm, these large tables are now rarely used for state visits. It was Jacqueline Kennedy who introduced the smaller, more intimate arrangement of tables for eight at state functions. This not only makes serving easier, but also allows for an artful, more natural gathering of guests based on interests and personalities.

This generic chart, created by White House staffers early in the Reagan administration, offers protocol guidelines for creating a guest list to a state dinner. "In the Reagan White House, the ultimate decision about who got invited came down to one thing," recalls Mike Deaver, former Deputy White House Chief of Staff. "What's in the best interest of the country?"

FAR RIGHT: An established hierarchy helps determine where people sit in relation to the president and first lady. Protocol also influences seating during entertainment in the East Room. Here, the final guest list of the Gorbachev state dinner is listed in order of protocol, with the President and Mrs. Reagan at the top.

Assistant Secretary of State and wife	2
Desk officer of country and wife	2
Chief of Protocol and wife	2
Secretary of State and wife	2
Official Party	12
	20

2	Supreme Court Justice and wife (rotating basis)
4	Two Cabinet Officers and wives (rotating basis)
8	Four Senator and Congressman couples
4	Two top military couples
2	One state governor or mayor couple
4	Two White House Special Assistant couples

24 total

The President and Mrs. Reagan	2
The Vice President and Mrs. Bush	2
couple suggested by Vice President	2
Four couples—Reagan friends or family	8
Two leading Washington couples (Mayor, head of Howard University, Smithsonian)	4
Two social Washington couples	4
Four contingency couples	8
Entertainers	4
	34

Compilation of State Dinner Guest Lists

100 total

ORDER OF PROTOCOL

THE PRESIDENT & MRS. REAGAN
Ms. Maureen Reagan & Mr. Dennis Revell

The Vice President & Mrs. Bush
The Speaker & Mrs. Wright
The Chief Justice & Mrs. Rehnquist
The Secretary of State & Mrs. Shultz
The Secretary of the Treasury & Mrs. Baker
The Secretary of Defense & Mrs. Carlucci
Hon. Howard H. Baker, Jr.
Hon. (Amb) Vernon A. Walters
Sen. & Mrs. Robert C. Byrd
Sen. & Mrs. Ted Stevens
Sen. Robert J. Dole & Hon. Elizabeth H. Dole
Rep. & Mrs. Robert H. Michel
Rep. Dick Cheney & Hon. Lynne V. Cheney
Hon. & Mrs. Kenneth M. Duberstein
Hon. & Mrs. Colin L. Powell
Hon. ~~& Mrs.~~ Henry A. Kissinger
Hon. & Mrs. Caspar W. Weinberger
Hon. (Amb) Max M. Kampelman
Hon. (Amb) Paul H. Nitze
Hon. & Mrs. Charles Z. Wick
Admiral & Mrs. William J. Crowe, Jr.
Amb. & Mrs. Jack F. Matlock, Jr.
The Chief of Protocol & Mr. Archibald B. Roosevelt, Jr.
Hon. Rozanne L. Ridgway & Captain Theodore Deming, USCG
Hon. Jeane J. Kirkpatrick & Dr. Evron M. Kirkpatrick
Hon. & Mrs. Zbigniew Brzezinski
Hon. & Mrs. Robert S. Strauss
Hon. & Mrs. Richard M. Helms
Hon. & Mrs. James H. Billington
Hon. J. Carter Brown
Hon. & Mrs. James D. Robinson III
Mr. & Mrs. Dwayne O. Andreas
Miss Pearl Bailey & Mr. Louis Bellson
Mr. Saul Bellow & Ms. Janis Freedman
Mr. & Mrs. Kenneth Bialkin
Mr. & Mrs. Dave Brubeck
Mrs. Ralph J. Bunche
Mr. Van Cliburn & Mrs. Rildia Bee Cliburn
Miss Claudette Colbert
Mr. Joe DiMaggio
Miss Chris Evert
Mr. Ted Graber
The Reverend & Mrs. Billy Graham
Dr. & Mrs. Armand Hammer
Mr. & Mrs. John H. Johnson
Mr. & Mrs. Robert G. Kaiser
Mr. & Mrs. Meadowlark Lemon
Mrs. Suzanne Massie
Maestro & Mrs. Zubin Mehta
Hon. & Mrs. Richard N. Perle
Mr. & Mrs. Donald E. Petersen
Miss Mary Lou Retton
Mr. & Mrs. David Rockefeller
Maestro & Mrs. Mstislav Rostropovich
Mr. & Mrs. Dimitri K. Simes
Mr. & Mrs. Hedrick Smith
Mr. & Mrs. Roger B. Smith
Mr. & Mrs. James Stewart
Ms. Kathleen Sullivan & Mr. Michael Kiner
Hon. Edward Teller
Mr. George Will

(handwritten list, left side)

One couple from the Arts (Museum directors head of Kennedy Center, Lincoln Center, etc.)	2
Two celebrity couples (movie or Broadway writer, sports stars, etc.)	4
Two fat cats couples (big contributors)	4
Two leading business couples (heads of major industries)	4
One labor couple	2
One couple from educational field (university president)	2
Two press couples	4

22 total

RIGHT: The Reagans share a cup of coffee with Shaikh Isa bin Sulman Al Khalifa, the emir of Bahrain, in the Blue Room in 1983. Visitors from most Middle Eastern countries shun alcohol at such events. The Protocol Office of the U.S. State Department informs the White House of any cultural differences or dietary requirements that will help the guest of honor feel welcome.

BOTTOM: President Reagan holds court at the head table in 1984. Premier Zhao Ziyang of the People's Republic of China, and the interpreter, sit to his right. When the leader is unaccompanied, it is accepted protocol for him or her to sit at the president's right, normally reserved for a spouse.

OPPOSITE: Reporters and their lights converge on the State Dining Room to record a toast during a 1984 state dinner. This necessary intrusion had the unintended effect of damaging the carefully staged ambiance. "The press would just tear it up," recalls former Chief Usher Gary Walters. During the second Reagan administration, Mrs. Reagan urged a change in protocol: thereafter, toasts would be made before dinner so as not to break the rhythm of the event.

PAGES 64–65: Mrs. Reagan and President Gorbachev toast each other at the beginning of this 1987 dinner at the Soviet embassy in Washington. Earlier, Soviet officials had called Colin Powell and said that a major problem was brewing. Powell expected a shift in policy or some other big crisis. The Soviets simply wanted to offer toasts at the beginning of the meal instead of at its conclusion. After a sigh of relief, Powell said, "Sure, let's do it." Powell's Soviet counterpart was stunned; wouldn't the Americans want to analyze this change in protocol to make sure it was not a diplomatic feint by the Kremlin? "I just told them the president would be fine with it," Powell recalls. Soon after this 1987 dinner, the White House began offering toasts at the start of the meal.

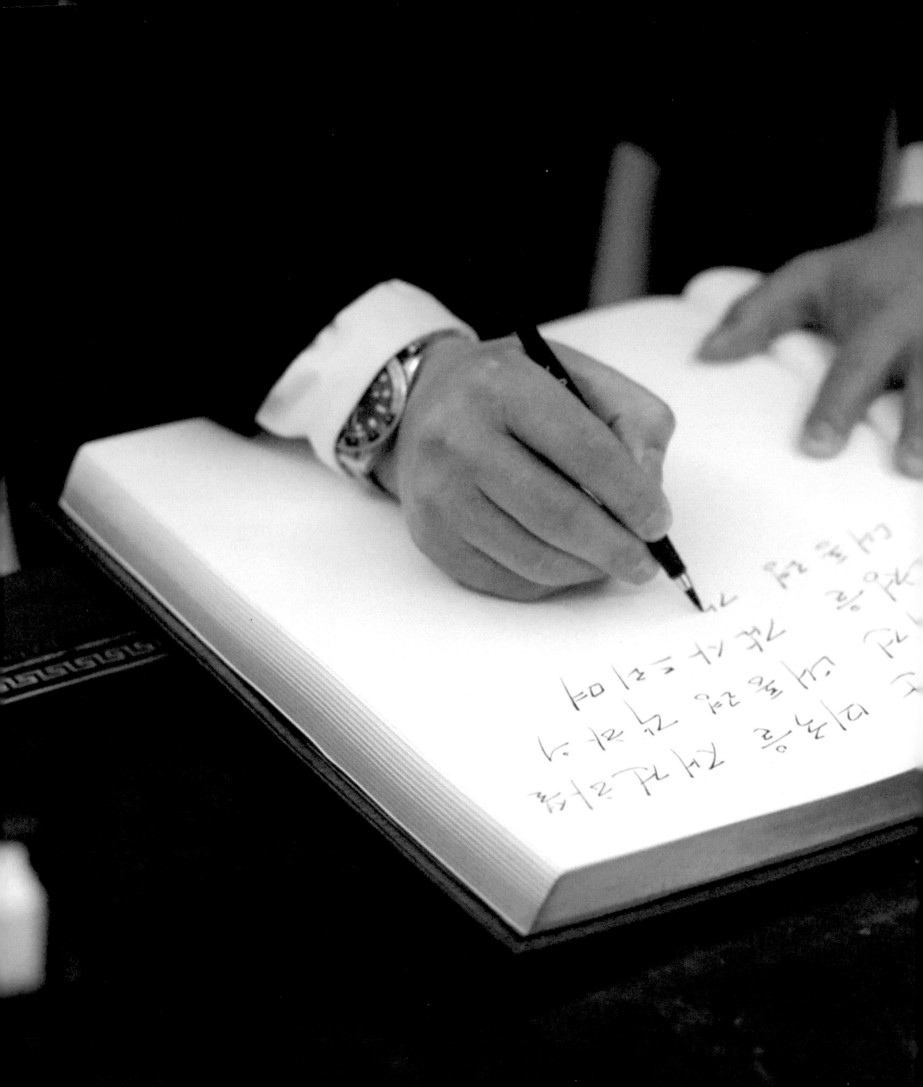

It is traditional for visitors to sign the White House guest book before state dinners commence. President Chun Doo Hwan of the Republic of Korea signs the Reagan guest book in the private quarters of the White House before a 1981 luncheon with the president.

CHAPTER THREE

Elements of Style

Elements of Style

ATTENTION TO DETAIL HAS BEEN AN INDISPENSABLE part of White House entertaining for more than two hundred years. The pageantry has unfolded with fresh flowers, good wines, and the best food served on the finest china. George Washington and many presidents selected their own china patterns, which remained the property of the White House and were used by those who followed. The careful selection of flowers and table settings constitutes more than good manners or the conceit of a wealthy nation. A White House that exudes warmth, style, and elegance helps bolster the public faith that the government is in good hands. "This is the President's House," observes Fred Ryan, longtime aide and friend to President Reagan. "Guests expect the very best that the country has to offer."

Yet for all its trappings of power, the White House still has some quaint touches. Its books and ledgers were kept in ink until the 1970s. Its kitchen is smaller than a ship's galley. Party tables and chairs are stacked neatly in hallways ready for use. Although the house was never intended to be a catering facility, it must accommodate receptions for up to five hundred people and host as many as five parties in a day. Year after year, the White House, guided by wise and professional ushers, serves the nation in grand style. "Everything you do has to be perfect," says former pastry chef Roland Mesnier. "There is no guessing or any 'second times.' There is no 'oops.' Perfection is no accident."

As usual, all goes well and the hard work fades into the background. Unknown to guests, for example, Chief Usher Gary Walters would stand in the doorway between the State and Family Dining Rooms and watch for cues from Mrs. Reagan. A slight nod indicated that they were ready for the next course. A look of concern informed Walters of an error by one of the nonstaff butlers.

"I was very busy then," Mrs. Reagan recalls. "We once held two dinners within five days of each other. The staff joked that if they'd been any closer together, they could have left the floral centerpieces on the tables."

Although matters pertaining to food and flowers may seem trivial in a swirl of global diplomacy, such details are scruti-nized. Perfection is its own reward, but a mistake can turn into a headline. A decision by the Reagan White House, for example, to serve a French burgundy to a group of editors and broadcasters created a stir. President Reagan, a fan and supporter of domestic wines, was criticized for offering a foreign wine at the White House even though President Nixon had purchased it years earlier.

"The table was large and rather handsome. The service was china. . . . The cloth, napkins, etc., etc., were fine and beautiful. The dinner was served in the French style and a little Americanized."

—JAMES FENIMORE COOPER at the Monroe White House, circa 1818

With so many other duties and issues to address, few presidents become involved with the ingredients of White House entertaining. President James Polk once looked askance at his dinner with an array of jellied meats and French delicacies and ordered a servant to bring him "a piece of cornbread and boiled ham." President Reagan, who enjoyed a simple steak or a bowl of chili, left these decisions to his wife. Some first ladies simply put their trust in the talented White House staff. "My social secretary would bring me menus and suggestions for entertainment," recalled Rosalyn Carter. "I would choose one. I was through."

The specifics of food, wine, and the pacing of dinners change with time. It is unlikely, for example, that the twenty-nine-course marathon feasts hosted by Mrs. Ulysses Grant will be repeated. Elaborate sauces, foie gras, and French pastries have given way to lighter fare delivered in four courses. Thomas Jefferson was an early believer in the health benefits of red wine. All spirits, including wine and beer, were banned during the administration of Rutherford B. Hayes. One official joked that at the Hayes White House "the water flowed like champagne." Wine was served for a formal dinner honoring the Grand Duke Alexis of Russia, but only after the president

was warned that "a dinner without wine would be an annoyance, if not an affront."

The staff is ready for almost anything at the White House. When President Lyndon Johnson said one morning to his wife, "Bird, let's have Congress over tonight," it was done. When Mrs. Reagan wanted a cabaret look for an East Room performance, White House carpenters built a set of floor risers to separate the dancers from the spectators. If a guest tears her dress on the dance floor, a seamstress is on hand to make repairs. "Everything is just so easy at the White House," recalls Letitia Baldrige, who helped both Jacqueline Kennedy and Nancy Reagan with social affairs.

"When I became first lady, one of the best pieces of advice I received was to simply be myself," recalls Mrs. Reagan. Her clarity and consistency were highly valued by the White House staff. "She expected the highest quality. She wanted the lights to be low, the flowers just right, and the service to be elegant. That's the kind romantic feeling she wanted attached to the White House," recalls Gary Walters. "The Reagan parties were always very elegant," observes former Secretary of State Colin Powell. "It was an American form of elegance."

LEFT: Mrs. Reagan's staff was careful to keep a record of where and when she had worn each gown. "It made my life much easier," she recalls. This official portrait by artist Aaron Shikler shows Mrs. Reagan in a gown designed by James Galanos.

PAGE 70: This 1967 table setting features American crystal made by Morgantown Glass Guild, Morgantown, West Virginia, and purchased by Jacqueline Kennedy in 1961.

PAGE 72: 1902 state dinner table setting for Prince Henry of Prussia, Theodore Roosevelt administration

TOP LEFT: Ida McKinley spent ten thousand dollars of her personal money on her wardrobe and diamond hair ornaments for her new role as first lady. Besieged by ill health, she spent much of her time secluded in her private quarters at the White House. When she did appear at state dinners and receptions, President McKinley broke protocol by sitting next to his wife to take care of her.

TOP RIGHT: Mrs. Julia Grant was a bit of a stickler for headwear. Women visiting the White House for afternoon receptions or teas were required to wear bonnets out of respect for the house. "Once in a while," she noted later, "a lady…would impose upon my good nature by attending without a bonnet…. This little maneuvering was never repeated by the same person." Thirty years later, an unctuous White House staffer banned the wearing of bonnets at evening events. Such is the fickle nature of White House fashion.

BOTTOM LEFT: Mary Todd Lincoln was criticized for her lavish spending on furniture, dress, and entertainment. Historian Catherine Allgor argues that the first lady knew that the perception of a shabby White House could nudge European governments into a pro-Confederate position. Thus the symbols of power, including entertainment, furnishings, and clothing, gave legitimacy to a president who was facing a revolt in the south.

BOTTOM RIGHT: First Lady Frances Folsom Cleveland shows off the latest fashion in gowns in 1886.

DINNER

Supreme of Pompano in Champagne
Fleurons

Roast Rack of Lamb Persillees
Fresh Mint Sauce
Vegetables Printanière

Hearts of Romaine Lettuce
Brie Cheese

Grand Marnier Soufflé

Beaulieu Vineyard Pinot Chardonnay
Inglenook Cabernet Sauvignon 1974
Schramsberg Blanc de Noirs

THE WHITE HOUSE
Thursday, February 26, 1981

DINNER

Cold Columbia River Salmon en Gelée
Dill Sauce

Suprême of Chicken Véronique
Wild Rice Amandine
Braised Endive

Bibb Lettuce Salad
Gourmandise Cheese
with Walnuts

Fantaisie of Pear Sorbet
in a Basket
Apricot Slices

Grgich Hills
Chardonnay 1979
Chalone Vineyard
Pinot Noir, Vin Gris 1980
Schramsberg
Crémant Demi-sec 1979

THE WHITE HOUSE
Tuesday, October 13, 1981

DINNER
Honoring
The Right Honorable
The Prime Minister of Canada
and Mrs. Mulroney

Smoked Salmon and Shrimp Mousse
Dilled Cucumber Sauce
Petits Corn Sticks

Roast Loin of Veal
Tarragon Sauce
Purée of Sweet Red Peppers
Spring Asparagus

Watercress and Radicchio Salad
Saint Paulin Cheese

Pineapple Champagne Sorbet
Petits Fours Sec

SILVERADO Chardonnay 1986
WILLIAMS SELYEM Pinot Noir 1985
S. ANDERSON Blanc de Noirs 1983

THE WHITE HOUSE
Wednesday, April 27, 1988

DINNER
In celebration of
The 200th Anniversary
of The White House

Truffle and Duck Consommé
Roasted Vegetables and Madeira
Seared Striped Bass
Corn and Crab Fricassee
Chive and Oyster Sauce
Grapefruit and Gin Sherbet
Smoked Loin of Lamb
Heirloom Apples, Butternut Squash and Salsify
Terrine of Pears, Figs and Wild Ripened Cheese
Winter Greens
Fig Dressing
Abigail Adams' Floating Island
Raisin Biscuits
Lemon Bars

Kistler Chardonnay "Cuvée Cathleen" 1996
Landmark Pinot Noir "Kastania Vineyard" 1997
Bonny Doon "Vin Glaciere Muscat" 1999

The White House
Thursday, November 9, 2000

LEFT: White House menus change with the times and the particular tastes of the president and first lady. A guest to a state dinner at the White House of Ulysses S. Grant, for example, would be treated to a feast of twenty-nine separate courses. Fortunately, that number has diminished over the years to a manageable four courses. It is customary for guests to pass the menus around the table for signatures. It is also common for guests to call the White House on the day after the party to request a menu from the dinner the night before, regretting that they had forgotten to take such a meaningful keepsake.

OPPOSITE: Mrs. Reagan had no great desire to buy new china for the White House. Breakage and pilfering, however, had left the house woefully in need of new plates and saucers. For their first state dinner in honor of Prime Minister Margaret Thatcher, Mrs. Reagan had to mix and match china from different administrations. "The press made it seem that I was trying to honor past leaders, which would have been a good idea," recalls Mrs. Reagan. "But the truth was that I did it because there simply wasn't enough of one pattern or presidency to make a complete setting." The amount spent on the new settings came entirely from private donations. This did not appease critics, who saw the china as a symbol of excess in a time of government austerity. The Reagan china, shown here awaiting guests to a state dinner, has been widely used and admired by every subsequent administration.

TOP ROW (LEFT TO RIGHT): Chinese export dinner plate from George Washington's administration; Benjamin Harrison breakfast plate; James Madison dinner plate; Woodrow Wilson dinner plate; Dwight D. Eisenhower china

BOTTOM ROW (LEFT TO RIGHT): Andrew Jackson dessert plate; Abraham Lincoln china; James Monroe dessert plate; Harry S. Truman dinner plate; Lyndon B. Johnson china

The hostess in this instance is Mrs. Reagan, who picked the Johnson china for a 1982 luncheon. Because of the limited number of services, the Johnson china is used mostly for luncheons and smaller occasions.

The White House chose the Eisenhower service for this 1998 state dinner. This is President Clinton's place at the table.

Mrs. Reagan worked closely with designers from Lenox China to achieve just the right tone for what has come to be known as "Reagan Red." Mrs. Reagan wanted a color that would have a strong presence in the off-white State Dining Room. "It is a very specific shade," observes Tim Carder, vice president of design at Lenox. "If the china is underfired, it becomes too purple. Overfire it, and it becomes too brown." The company created sixty services in addition to the three hundred that were ordered and selected the best of the lot for the White House.

TOP LEFT: A table set for the Gorbachev Dinner.

BOTTOM LEFT: A table awaits guests in the Family Dining Room for a private dinner for Princess Margaret in 1983.

TOP RIGHT: A table set for the president's seventieth birthday party boasts the celadon-rimmed Truman china against a light blue tablecloth. When not in use, the gold banquet chairs are stacked neatly in a small storage room on the ground floor of the White House.

BOTTOM RIGHT: The Truman china is used for a simple luncheon for Prince Phillip in the solarium on the top floor of the White House. The solarium is a modern, bright room and a favorite of most presidents. It is relatively informal compared to the antique-laden rooms on the lower floors of the White House.

TOP LEFT: For the state dinner honoring Prime Minister Brian Mulroney of Canada, florists placed cherry blossom branches in the eye line of guests, but made sure that they were sparse enough not to inhibit cross-table banter. Note the blending of pinks and red in the table setting. The White House staff prefers tall candles to provide illumination that is more flattering to the guests.

BOTTOM LEFT: A luncheon for the Prime Minister of Jamaica in 1981, the Reagan's first state visit, featured the Johnson china. Its delicate beauty and colors depicting the wildflowers of Texas make it a White House favorite.

TOP RIGHT: The Truman china was used for this 1965 luncheon.

BOTTOM RIGHT: A table set for the annual Governors' Dinner in 1982, using the Johnson china and a mix of silver and vermeil flatware.

An all-white arrangement featuring rubrum lilies, tulips, snapdragons, pussy willows, and white amaryllis.

A harmony of pinks and whites with dianthus, tulips, snapdragons, and delphiniums.

ABOVE: David Jones, a celebrated Los Angeles floral designer and friend of Mrs. Reagan's, traveled east to design the floral arrangements for the 1984 state dinner in honor of Premier Zhao Ziyang of the People's Republic of China. Jones used small pineapples as the focal point to the dramatic centerpieces. "The White House staff was wonderful," he recalls. "To imagine that they held state dinners almost once a month is just amazing."

TOP RIGHT: Each first lady has had a favorite flower and it is often used as the centerpiece of major dinners. Mrs. Reagan loves peonies, so much so that she would sometimes request them when they were not available. "When she left the White House, I embroidered her a pillow that said 'Peonies Bloom in May,'" recalls White House florist Nancy Clarke, shown here in the ground floor florist's shop of the White House.

BOTTOM RIGHT: A White House florist finishes an arrangement for a state dinner honoring Prime Minister Malcolm Fraser of Australia in 1981. The florists try to coordinate the flowers with the room, the china, and the menu. "We have such a range of colors to work with that it's rarely a problem," says florist Nancy Clarke.

OVERLEAF: Mrs. Reagan preferred a more natural arrangement of flowers, such as the white lilies draped over a mantelpiece in the East Room for the Gorbachev state dinner in 1987. Such an arrangement would never be used for a visit from an Asian country, where the color white is associated with death and mourning.

ABOVE: This flatware from the International Silver Co. was first used in 1926 by Calvin Coolidge.

OPPOSITE TOP: These gilded silver spoons were used during the administration of Martin Van Buren.

OPPOSITE BOTTOM: A family history is intricately carved on this spoon, inherited by Thomas Jefferson through his marriage to Martha Wayles Skelton, who died in 1782.

This spoon belonged to Thomas Jefferson 3rd President of the United States and was in constant use at Monticello. It came to him upon his marriage Jan. 1st 1772 with Martha Wales dau. of John Wales and widow of Bathurst Skelton.

It was made in London in 1768-9 and decended to Jefferson's eldest dau. Martha wife of Gov. Thos. Mann Randolph, to her son Col. Thos. Jeff Randolph to his son Major Thos. Jeff Randolph and finally to his son Mr T. M. Randolph of Keswick Albemarle Co. Va. Jefferson's great greatgrandson, from whom it passed Dec. 1884 to General Meredith Read whose great grandfather George Read of Delaware the Signer, was colleague of Mr Jefferson in the Continental Congress. The letters B. M. S. stand for Bathurst & Martha Skelton.

This large trunk holds a set of silver made in France and purchased
by Andrew Jackson in 1833.

The elegant style of the White House is shown with a silver
breakfast tray served to President Theodore Roosevelt, circa 1905.

American crystal made by T. G. Hawkes & Company, Corning, New York, ordered by President and Mrs. Franklin Roosevelt in 1937.

Given to the White House in 1981 by Mr. and Mrs. Stanley F. Reed, this set of American crystal, made in 1932 by Steuben Glass, Corning, New York, was designed by Frederick Carder.

TOP AND BOTTOM: Most first ladies leave menu details to their social secretaries. Nancy Reagan liked to test each menu before state dinners. After sampling the meal, she would meet with the White House chef to discuss any change or recommendations. After several years of hearing Mrs. Reagan's likes and dislikes, Chef Henry Haller, shown at left, knew how to create a meal that would please the first lady. "We've done a lot better because we know what she wants," Haller has said. "Smaller portions, different color combinations. The platters we make are fancier. We spend more time on them. We take pictures with a Polaroid so the staff knows how they are to be done. With the Reagans you have to be more creative."

OPPOSITE: A busy staff works in the cramped quarters of the White House kitchen, preparing gourmet food for up to 140 guests. "Menus are based on what the first lady and chef want for the dinner," says Gary Walters, former White House usher. "I can't think of a single time we've rejected a menu because of the size of the kitchen. We've gone outside to smoke a turkey, but that's it." New chefs interviewing for coveted White House jobs are often stunned by the small size of the kitchen. A common refrain from the uninitiated: "You've got to be kidding me. Where's the other kitchen?"

To make biscuit de Savoye.

12 eggs. —
12 table spoonfuls of sugar
separate the yolk & white perfectly
grate the peel of one orange.
mix the whole, & beat them very well.
6 spoonfuls of flour, put thro' a searce.
beat well the whites separately.
mix the whole gently.
grease the mould with butter.
powder it with sugar.
put in the mixture & put it in
the oven. of the same heat as that
used in the case of the Macarons
take care not to shut the oven till
the biscuit begins to swell up.
then close the oven.
a half an hour suffices to bake
more or less according to size.

Blanc Manger.

4 oz. sweet almonds, with 5 or 6 bitter
almonds. pour boiling water on them
to take off the skin.
put them in a mortar & beat them
with a little cream.
take them out of the mortar & liquify
them with cream little by little (perhaps a
pou) stirring them.
4 oz sugar now to be put in.
having dissolved some
isinglass (colle de poisson)
say 1 oz. in boiling water & pour it
into the preceding mixture, mean
stirring them well together.
strain it thro' a napkin
put it into a mould, & it is done.

Vine jellies.

take 4 calves feet & wash them well
without taking off the hoofs. (or instead of that 1 oz. isinglass, or 1 oz.
of dears horns)
these feet must be well boiled the
day before they are wanted.
let them cool in order to take off the grease
after taking off the grease put the jelly
in a casserolle. put there 4 oz. sugar
cloves, nutmeg, boil all together.
take 6. whites of eggs, the juice of 6 le-
mons, a pint of milk, a pint of madeira
stir all together.
pour it into the jelly & boil it.
strain the whole thro' flannel.
taste it to see if sweet enough, if
not, add powdered sugar.
strain it 2 or 3 times thro' flan-
-nel till clear.
put it in glasses or moulds.

Ice cream.

2 bottles of good cream.
6 yolks of eggs.
½ lb sugar
mix the yolks & sugar
put the cream on a fire in a casse-
-role, first putting in a stick of vanilla
then near boiling take it off
pour it gently into the mixture
of eggs & sugar.
stir it well.
put it on the fire again stirring
it throughly with a spoon to
prevent it's sticking to the casse-
-role.
then near boiling take it off and
strain it thro' the tamis.
then set it in ice an hour before
it is to be served. put into the
ice a handful of salt,
put ice all round the Sabotiere.
i.e. a layer of ice a layer of salt
for three layers.
put salt on the cover lid of the
Sabotiere & cover the whole with
ice.
leave it still half a quarter of an
hour.
then turn the Sabotiere in the
ice 10 minutes.
open it to loosen with a spatula
the ice from the inner sides of
the Sabotiere.
shut it & replace it in the ice.
open it from time to time to de-
-tach the ice from the sides.
when well taken (prise) stir it
well with the Spatule.
put it in moulds, justling it
well down on the knee.
then put the mould into the
same bucket of ice.
leave it there to the moment
of serving it.
to withdraw it, immerse the
mould in warm water,
turning it well till it
will come out & turn it
into a plate.

Meringues

12 blancs d'oeuf
les fouetter bien ferme
12 cueillerées de sucre en p
put them by little & little into the
whites of eggs
fouetter le tout ensemble
dresser les sur un papier à
un cueiller de bouche
mettre les dans un four bien
doux, that is to say in a
oven after the bread is
out. you may leave
there as long as you p

Macarons

pour boiling water on your
ammonds & take off the sk
put with them in cold wat
wipe them well in a towel
beat them
add whites of eggs from time to time
beating them always, to
prevent their turning into
oil.
take them out of the mortar
add sugar & whites of eggs.
beat them well with a wood-
-en spoon.
then taste the paste to see
if it is not too bitter
add sugar if you find it too b
dresser les avec deux cou
by the grosseur d'un noise
des feuilles de papier.
put them in an oven not too
but hotter than after taking
out the bread.
you prove the proper heat of
oven by holding in it a lit
white paper. if it burns, it
burns your macarons, if it
just browns the paper it is
exact.

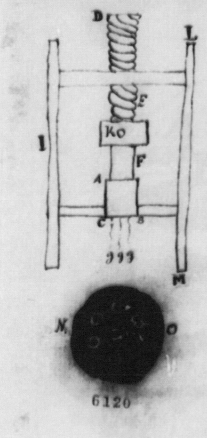

Maccaroni.

The best maccaroni in Italy is made with a particular sort of flour called Semola, in Naples: but in almost every shop a different sort of flour is commonly used; for, provided the flour be of a good quality & not ground extremely fine, it will always do very well. a paste is made with flour, water & less yeast than is used for making bread. this paste is then put, by little at a time, viz. about 5. or 6.℔ each time into a round iron box ABC. the under part of which is perforated with holes, through which the paste, when pressed by the screw DEF, comes out, and forms the Maccaroni g.g.g. which, when sufficiently long, are cut & spread to dry. the screw is turned by a lever inserted into the hole K. of which there are 4. or 6. it is evident that on turning the screw one way, the cylindrical part F which fits the iron box or mortar perfectly well, must press upon the paste and must force it out of the holes. I.I.M. is a strong wooden frame, properly fast-ened to the wall, floor & cieling of the room.

N.O is a figure, on a larger scale, of some of the holes in the iron plate, where all the black is solid, and the rest open. the real plate has a great many holes, and is screwed to the box or mortar: or rather there is a set of plates which may be changed at will, with holes of different shapes & sizes for the different sorts of Maccaroni.

THOMAS JEFFERSON

Although he is sometimes given credit, incorrectly, for introducing ice cream to America, there is no doubt that Thomas Jefferson helped spread its popularity. Opposite, second from left, Jefferson jotted down this recipe for ice cream to be served in warm puff pastry. Jefferson was the first great gourmand in the White House and kept detailed records related to his many interests, including the collection of recipes and inventions such as the macaroni machine, shown above. Entertaining was expensive even in 1801. Jefferson would often spend fifty dollars in a day when a whole turkey cost less than a dollar. His guests were thrilled with exotic dishes such as waffles and macaroni.

Dolly Johnson, a cook during the Benjamin Harrison administration, had help from a number of conveniences, including a drying rack and a coal range. Johnson, a black woman from Kentucky, was hired by First Lady Caroline Harrison to prepare simple, wholesome meals for the first family. The previous chef had been fired for insisting upon heavy sauces and pastries that did not agree with either the first lady or the president. Johnson earned fifteen dollars a month for her efforts. She is shown in 1888 in the smaller of two kitchens along the northwest corner of the ground floor. This kitchen, used mostly for the president and his family, is now a pantry adjacent to the main kitchen.

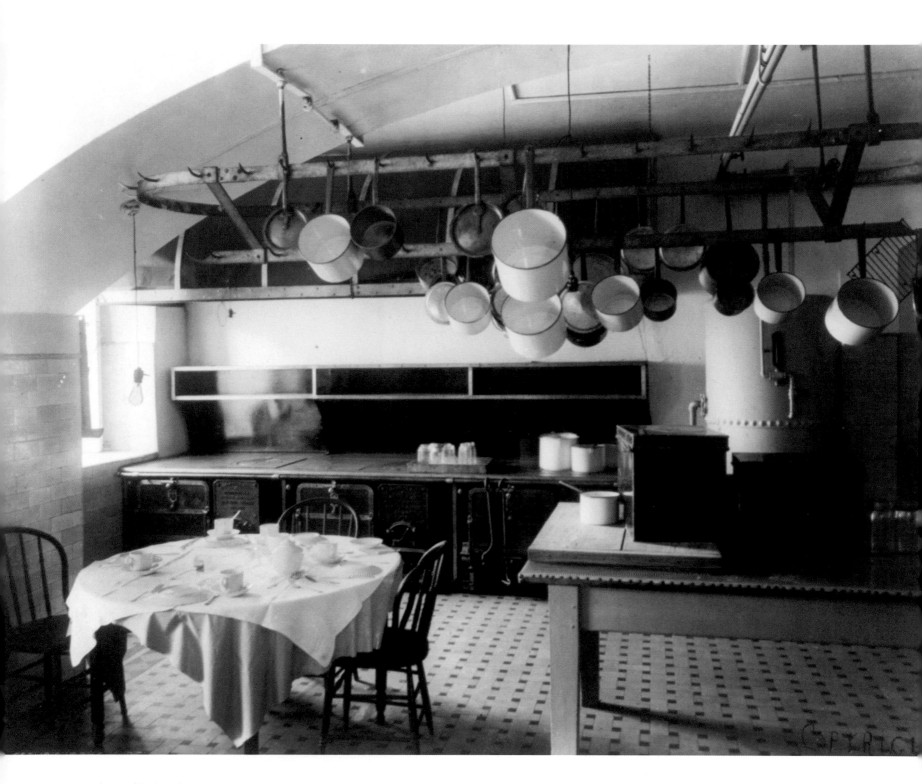

A larger kitchen in the center of the ground floor was used for public dinners and receptions. It was here that Thomas Jefferson installed the first cooking range, which probably burned coal. Dolley Madison's chefs would later use the stove to prepare ice cream balls in puff pastry. The White House stoves still used coal when this photograph was taken in 1901.

By the time Eleanor Roosevelt took her first tour of her new home in 1933, the kitchen had become rundown. "This was the 'First Kitchen,'" wrote Henrietta Nesbitt, the housekeeper during the Roosevelt years. "And it wasn't even sanitary. Mrs. Roosevelt and I poked around, opening doors and expecting hinges to fall off and things to fly out."

ABOVE: The small family kitchen in the northwest corner of the ground floor is shown in 1904. Franklin Roosevelt, who intensely disliked the food prepared by the White House chef, would later have a small kitchen built in the private quarters to prepare meals more to his taste.

OPPOSITE: A renovation during the Theodore Roosevelt administration added glass cabinetry to the large kitchen on the ground floor of the White House. The cabinets have long since been replaced by stainless steel, but the current kitchen is in the same location. Although small for the demands it must meet, the kitchen is renowned for its ergonomic efficiency. After the bicentennial celebrations in 1976, more events were held at the White House. The kitchen became a catering facility that had to service events both small and large. Yet the kitchen's dimensions have remained largely the same. "There's no such thing as a room-stretcher," says former chief usher Gary Walters.

CHAPTER FOUR

Private Gatherings

Private Gatherings

IS IT DIFFICULT TO THROW A SURPRISE PARTY FOR THE Commander-in-Chief? "Everything was fine until that morning," recalls Mrs. Reagan of her 1981 premiere as a White House hostess. "We were watching the *Today* show and there was Tom Brokaw saying 'Mrs. Reagan has been planning a surprise seventieth birthday party for her husband.' I turned to Ronnie and said, 'The press exaggerates everything. They make such a big deal out of a little dinner with ten people.'" That night, President Reagan was greeted by dozens of close friends, including Frank Sinatra and Jimmy Stewart, who came for the black tie event.

The celebration was the first of many private parties held by President and Mrs. Reagan. From casual picnics around the pool to black tie events that made headlines around the world, the president and first lady enjoyed sharing the grandeur of the White House with friends and family. Even when Mrs. Reagan had to leave the White House for campaign treks or other business, she would arrange small dinner parties in the Red Room for her husband and twenty friends. "These kind of parties were important to the Reagans," recalls former Chief Usher Gary Walters. "There were always friendly faces at the Reagan White House."

Most presidents and their wives have enjoyed such moments. Chester Arthur, a bon vivant among presidents, held stag parties with fine wines, fourteen courses, and the best cigars. Ulysses S. Grant spent hours hunched over a billiards table with Civil War comrades. Eleanor Roosevelt gathered some of the finest minds of her day around the table in the Family Dining Room, where she would scramble eggs in a chafing dish. In light of the guest list, the staff referred to the Sunday luncheons as "scrambled eggs with brains." Harry Truman enjoyed a game of poker and a drink with friends and, when asked about his choice of liquor, announced proudly, "Kentucky bourbon."

In truth, there is little that happens in the White House that is not subject to public scrutiny. One might not think that an elegant party for Prince Charles and Princess Diana, announced on front pages around the world, is a private affair.

But there are important distinctions, both politically and financially, between a public and private gathering. In the language of protocol, *private* means that the government will not pay for the food, wine, or extra staff needed to entertain. Nor will the office of protocol or White House officials have any real say regarding guest lists or other details. Out of courtesy, the protocol office will offer advice on visits from foreign dignitaries and royalty. The scope of their involvement, however, is greatly curtailed.

This scenario offers a clear advantage to a first lady. Freed from constraints of protocol, she can rely solely upon her instincts as a hostess to create guests lists, menus, and select entertainment. As a result, private parties are often more lively, casual, and eclectic than state dinners, where concerns of etiquette and hierarchy are paramount. There are disadvantages as well. For one, the president and first lady must pay all expenses. In addition, while a first lady has greater leeway in selecting guests for private parties, she also runs a greater risk of offending those who do not make the list.

It is axiomatic that the smaller the number of guests, the greater the honor of a White House invitation. Entrée into a small gathering in the private quarters of the White House is the pinnacle of Washington society. The private party for Prince Charles was the first gathering hosted by the Reagans after the 1981 assassination attempt on the president. Audrey Hepburn, Cary Grant, and author William F. Buckley Jr. were among the guests. Before dinner, guests to such small gatherings normally gather in the Yellow Room for a cocktail. President Reagan's preference was consistent over the years; the butlers knew exactly how he liked his light beverage of orange juice with a splash of vodka. Mrs. Reagan would choose white wine or a simple glass of mineral water. In the president's dining room in the private quarters of the White House—which is impractical for large state functions, but perfect for intimate gatherings—the staff will often set up four round tables to accommodate up to thirty-five guests. For small gatherings such as these, Mrs. Reagan often selected antique crystal and flatware with mother-of-pearl handles from the White House collection. The staff takes great pride, however, in treating everyone equally. The menu and wines for Prince Charles or Crown Prince Akihito are very much the same as for guests to other state dinners and formal occasions. Every guest is treated like royalty.

In the early months of his administration, President Reagan seemed charmingly unfamiliar with the workings of what he would later call the "Five-Star Hotel." In 1981, presidential aide Mike Deaver was on hand for a private birthday celebration for Speaker of the House Tip O'Neil. When a cake was about to be served, the president turned to a butler and asked, innocently, "Do you think there might be a bottle of champagne in the White House?"

"Yes, Mr. President," the butler answered. "I believe there is."

Even in such intimate settings, surrounded by close friends, President and Mrs. Reagan retained the aura and dignity of the office. In a word, they remained "presidential" at all times, even with old friends like Cary Grant and Douglas Fairbanks. "President Reagan had a preternatural affability which I believe was a way of maintaining his privacy," observes columnist and historian George Will. "He was a very complex, private man and not the 'hail fellow well met' that he appeared to be."

Guests at Ronald Reagan's table would often be treated to stories from his Hollywood days. He was gracious enough to know that his guests expected him to entertain, and he obliged with both prose and poetry. The president would rarely discuss himself, however, or allow a conversation to become too intimate. Yet his guests came away with a sense of warmth and integrity. "It didn't make a bit of difference who you were," recalls Mike Deaver. "If you were talking to President Reagan, he made you feel that you were the most important person in the room."

PAGE 102: Guests gather in the Yellow Room during a 1983 dinner for Princess Margaret of Great Britain.

PAGE 104: President Reagan greets Leonore and Walter Annenberg in the East Room during the President's surprise seventieth birthday party. Mrs. Annenberg, a longtime friend of the Reagans, had just been named chief of protocol in 1981.

RIGHT: Mother Teresa visits with Mrs. Reagan in 1981. President Reagan was asked about what he said to the Nobel Prize–winning nun. "I listened," Reagan answered. Mother Teresa was awarded the Presidential Medal of Freedom by Reagan in 1985.

TOP: Mrs. Reagan and Queen Sofia of Spain in 1986 share tea while White House pet Cavalier King Charles spaniel "Rex" scampers under the table.

BOTTOM: Prince Charles signs the guest book during his first visit to the White House in 1981.

OPPOSITE: Mrs. Reagan introduces Prince Charles to fashion icon Diana Vreeland at a private dinner for the prince in 1981.

TOP: Singer Bobby Short entertains a small group of guests in the Yellow Oval Room during Prince Charles's first visit to the Reagan White House. The room is often used for small recitals and performances.

BOTTOM: Cellist Yo-Yo Ma performs for Crown Prince Akihito and Princess Michiko of Japan.

OPPOSITE: Nancy Reagan and Elizabeth Taylor chat before the start of a small dinner for Crown Prince Akihito and Crown Princess Michiko in 1987.

ABOVE: Celebrated actress Helen Hayes joins Nancy Reagan for tea in the Yellow Room. Hayes was called the first lady of the American theater.

OPPOSITE: President and Mrs. Reagan greet Prince Charles and Princess Diana upstairs at the White House in 1985. The private party for the royal couple was one of the most highly anticipated events of the Reagan administration.

ABOVE: Presidential aide Mike Deaver shows off his steps to Maureen Reagan, President Reagan's daughter, as Carol Price and Jack Hume strike a more dignified pose.

RIGHT: President and Mrs. Reagan share a dance at the surprise party for Ronald Reagan's seventieth birthday. The Reagans' closest friends and loyal supporters attended the private celebration. "It was a marvelous party," recalls Leonore Annenberg.

A Celebrated Dance

It took a good deal of advance work to create these iconic images. Weeks before Princess Diana and Prince Charles visited the White House in 1985, Mrs. Reagan had asked her staff about potential dance partners for the visiting princess. Social secretary Gahl Hodges Burt had met John Travolta months earlier. Mrs. Reagan and Hodges Burt considered him a perfect dance partner. With the help of producer Robert Stigwood, Travolta was invited to the small party for the royal couple. The Marine Band had prepared for the moment by practicing "Stayin' Alive," the disco tune that helped make Travolta famous. At the appointed moment, Mrs. Reagan urged Travolta to cut in on Princess Diana and President Reagan, who was in on the surprise arrangement. In a rare show of respect for a nonroyal, Princes Diana curtsied to Travolta at the end of their dance.

ABOVE: President Reagan greets Audrey Hepburn and Rob Wolders during a private dinner for Prince Charles.

OPPOSITE: President Reagan welcomes Betsy Bloomingdale at the private party for Prince Charles and Princess Diana in 1985. This White House party was the most coveted event of the Reagan years. Bloomingdale recalls that entertaining helped the Reagans win over an East Coast establishment wary of Westerners in the White House. "I can remember that they thought, 'Those Californians, they don't know anything.' But the Reagans surprised them. Everything was so beautifully done. After a while, the old guard in Washington had to admit that they turned out to be pretty good."

LEFT: President Reagan greets Cary Grant and Douglas Fairbanks Jr. in the Yellow Room. Grant was a favorite of the White House staff. "He was exactly what you'd hope Cary Grant would be like," recalls social secretary Linda Faulkner. "A real gentleman." At one small party, Grant realized that guests were not leaving as early as they should. "I'll go," Grant said to Faulkner. "Maybe I'll get something started." Mrs. Reagan was grateful. Diagnosed with breast cancer earlier that day, she had gone ahead bravely with the party as scheduled.

BOTTOM LEFT: Dancer Mikhail Baryshnikov lights a cigarette while chatting with former Ambassador Walter Annenberg. Administrations have differed on their policies toward tobacco. Until President and Mrs. Clinton banned it outright, most administrations tolerated its use. During the Reagan presidency, White House staff supplied guests with matches, ashtrays, and six different kinds of cigarettes held in crystal vases. Although smoking is now forbidden, White House matches are still distributed as keepsakes.

OPPOSITE: President Reagan chats with Jimmy Stewart in the East Room during the president's seventieth birthday party.

President Reagan shares a laugh in 1986 with Hume Cronyn,
Lucille Ball, Mrs. Reagan, Ray Charles, Yehudi Menuhin, and
others at a reception in the Green Room. The performers had just
been awarded the Kennedy Center Honors.

The Reagans held frequent gatherings in the small movie theater near the East Entrance to the White House. Here, Mrs. Reagan chats with Warren Beatty and Diane Keaton during a 1981 screening of *Reds*. Franklin D. Roosevelt added the movie theater to the White House in 1942, and presidents have since used it for entertaining guests.

ABOVE: President and Mrs. Reagan share a laugh with guests during a casual pool party in 1981. The pool was built in 1975 by President Gerald Ford. Future Secretary of Staff James Baker is at the left and Deputy White House Chief of Staff Mike Deaver is seated behind the first lady.

OPPOSITE: President Reagan chats over a cocktail with Frank Sinatra on a spring evening in 1981. President Harry Truman angered architects by installing a balcony overlooking the south lawn in 1947. After the assassination attempt on Ronald Reagan, the balcony was used more cautiously.

CHAPTER FIVE

Celebrations

Celebrations

JUST ACROSS THE SOUTH LAWN FROM THE WHITE house, a forty-foot Colorado blue spruce tree stands in the center of the area known as the Ellipse. Every December, the president throws a switch to illuminate thousands of colored lights on the tree. Since its debut in 1923, the National Christmas Tree has become a herald of the holiday season. In times of strife or sorrow, presidents have elected to dim its lights as a symbol of respect. During World War II, fear of air attacks kept the lights off for two years. In 1963 President Johnson postponed lighting the tree for thirty days of mourning in the wake of President Kennedy's assassination. President Carter lit the tree for only 417 seconds—one second for each day that the hostages had been held at the U.S. embassy in Tehran. On January 20, 1981, in one of the earliest and most joyful duties of his administration, President Reagan lit the tree to celebrate the long-sought release of the hostages.

The National Christmas Tree is the most visible sign of a White House that takes its celebrations seriously. From New Year's Day to New Year's Eve, holidays and homecomings provide Americans with the opportunity to visit the house at the height of its beauty. Smaller occasions such as staff birthdays are also cause for celebration among the tight-knit White House family. At the heart of the celebrations are the children who gather on the South Lawn or in the Blue Room for various parties throughout the year. "The White House is at its best when children are there," says Mrs. Reagan. "A great deal of our planning for the holidays was to insure that children had a wonderful time visiting the house."

On the Monday after every Easter, for example, youngsters crowd the South Lawn to participate in the grand American tradition of the White House Easter Egg Roll. In 1878, a mob of children reportedly pushed against White House gates to protest legislation that would ban them from the South Lawn. President Rutherford B. Hayes allowed them in and the tradition of the Easter Egg Roll took hold. By the beginning of Calvin Coolidge's administration, the Easter Egg Roll resembled a festive demolition derby. It was a favorite day for First Lady Grace Coolidge, who charmed children by introducing them to Rebecca, her pet raccoon.

In 1981 President and Mrs. Reagan put their stamp of approval on the yearly event by hosting a hunt for colorfully decorated wooden eggs that had been signed by celebrities and high-ranking White House officials. The tradition continues today, with eggs from each of the fifty states represented alongside the hundreds of VIP eggs hidden on the South Lawn. The eggs, given only to children under twelve years old, are now treasured keepsakes of the Easter celebration and are inscribed with the signatures of the president and first lady.

Long before the first egg is rolled, planning for the winter holidays has begun. New first ladies are often surprised when, shortly after inauguration, the chief usher takes them aside and asks about plans for Christmas, still ten months away. By the time Christmas arrives, some two dozen trees will be trimmed. More than twenty-five thousand lights will be installed on trees throughout the house, and eight thousand ornaments hung. Lighting the National Christmas Tree has become part of the Pageant of Peace, which includes choir and gospel groups, strolling performers, and bell ringers. Lesser known, but just as vital to millions of Americans, is the White House celebration of Hanukkah. Each year, a giant menorah and its thirty-foot electric candles grace Lafayette Park on the north side of the house. Holiday cards are sent to thousands of friends and supporters.

The kitchen bustles as well. White House chefs have learned to provide six pastries for every guest at the dozens of parties held over the holidays; a good number of the desserts have a way of slipping into the pockets of guests to be used later as Christmas ornaments.

The arrival of the official White House tree, which decorates the Blue Room, is in itself cause for celebration. Chosen from thousands of trees from across the nation, the tree arrives by horse-drawn cart during the first week of December. In 1986 the tree was graced with miniature ceramic geese and fifteen characters from the Mother Goose rhymes. Upstairs in the private quarters, President and Mrs. Reagan preferred to decorate their tree simply, with popcorn and family ornaments, including ones made by their children while they were in elementary school.

Many holiday decorations made repeat appearances at the Reagan White House. One of Mrs. Reagan's favorites was a train that, with the help of its teddy bear conductor, circled the perimeter of the tree in the Blue Room. Another mainstay was an elaborate gingerbread house created by chef Hans Raffert. It was three feet tall and decorated with jellybeans, candy canes, white icing, and chocolate cookies. It presented a challenge to White House staffers when they had to move it carefully from the pastry kitchen to a mantle in the State Dining Room without a collapse. "It was nerve-racking, but we made it," recalls chief usher Gary Walters. In addition to the White House staff, dozens of volunteers from around the country spend days helping with the decorations.

Between Thanksgiving and New Year's Day, there are often as many as five parties a day. It is a chance for all those who contribute to the White House to bring wives, husbands, and children into the brilliantly decorated home. The president and first lady host parties for the military, the Secret Service, congressmen, and senior citizens, among many others. The residential staff, including the butlers, chambermaids, carpenters, and chefs who keep the house in order are also given a party. One of the most anticipated parties is held for the children of diplomats from around the world who work and live in Washington. Even reporters, regardless of their position vis-à-vis the current administration, are welcomed for several parties. In 1988, celebrating her last holiday in the White House, Nancy Reagan gave a tour of the decorations to a press group. Teary and sentimental, Mrs. Reagan joked, "You won't believe this, but I'm even going to miss you."

No holiday is more closely associated with the White House than the Fourth of July. John Adams had predicted that the holiday would be celebrated "with pomp and parades . . . shows and games . . . and sports and guns and bells . . . with bonfires and illuminations, from one end of this continent to the other, and from this time forevermore." Thomas Jefferson (who, as author of the Declaration of Independence, was celebrating his own work) hosted the first White House celebration in 1801. In 1861 Abraham Lincoln inspected twenty thousand soldiers from New York regiments as they marched past the White House in the early days of the Civil War.

Their first White House Fourth of July had special significance for President and Mrs. Reagan. Gathered with friends and staff, they were able to take in the view of fireworks over the Washington Mall and celebrate the president's return to health after an assassination attempt three months earlier. "It was a special night for my husband and me," Mrs. Reagan recalls. "There's really no better place to spend a holiday than at the White House."

The President and Mrs. Reagan
extend to you their warmest wishes
for a joyous holiday season
and a happy new year.

1986

ABOVE: The Reagan's 1986 card, by artist Thomas William Jones.

OPPOSITE: The 1983 tree was decorated with dozens of antique toys from the Strong Museum in Rochester, New York.

PAGE 128: The national Christmas tree, 1965.

PAGE 130: The President and Mrs. Reagan, Christmas 1983.

Calvin and Grace Coolidge sent out the first White House Christmas cards, but it was not until 1953 with President Eisenhower that the tradition became an official duty of the White House.

TOP: The 1935 card from Franklin and Eleanor Roosevelt.

MIDDLE: The 1967 card from President and Mrs. Johnson, by artist Robert Laessig.

BOTTOM FAR AND NEAR LEFT: The 1962 and 1963 cards from John F. Kennnedy.

OPPOSITE: The 1981 card from the Reagan White House, painted by Jamie Wyeth.

ABOVE: Children gather around the tree in the East Room in 1934. The first Christmas tree in the White House was trimmed with only white candles by First Lady Caroline Harrison in 1889.

OPPOSITE: A group of flocked trees grace the East Room in 1985. Hundreds of small white lights, artificial snow, and glass icicles were used. Ever since Mrs. Herbert Hoover first established the custom of an official White House tree in 1929, each first lady has had the honor of overseeing the tree trimming.

ABOVE LEFT: It is traditional for the official White House tree to be placed in the Blue Room, which is in the center of the house on the public floor. Workmen must first remove the chandelier to accommodate the twenty-foot-high spruce, fir, or pine tree. The Blue Room tree, such as this one in 1984, usually arrives at the White House in the first week of December.

ABOVE RIGHT: For the Christmas tree in 1981, the White House borrowed dozens of handmade tree ornaments from the American Folk Art Museum in New York.

OPPOSITE: In 1982, Mrs. Reagan asked volunteers from the Second Genesis rehabilitation program to help with the decoration of this tree. The Origami Society of New York created one hundred ornaments wrapped in velvet and lace. The young people worked with the florist's office and were later invited to the Christmas party for volunteers.

Nancy Reagan joins television personality Willard Scott as Santa Claus at a reception for the children of foreign diplomats in 1987.

William Gemmell, the White House director of the Graphics and Calligraphy office, executed the sketches, opposite, for these decorations.

Legendary musical comedy star Mary Martin performs with a group of young singers during one of the *In Performance at the White House* series.

"Annie" (Andrea McCardle) entertains Mrs. Reagan and her
guests during a Christmas reception for the children of foreign
diplomats in 1982. The White House hosts dozens of receptions
and large parties between Thanksgiving and New Year's Day.
Many of the events feature children as the guests of honor.

The splendor of Christmas at the White House would not be possible were it not for the dozens of volunteers from around the country who spend many hours helping with the decorations, including the trimming of some twenty trees spread throughout the mansion. The volunteers work alongside White House florists and other staff members to create up to seventy-five wreaths from boughs of evergreen trees. Hundreds of red and white poinsettias are spread through both public and private rooms. Chandeliers are decorated with swags of evergreens, gold bulbs, and bright red ribbons. Planning for all of this begins shortly after the end of the previous Christmas holiday.

OPPOSITE: Nancy Reagan on the Grand Staircase in December 1982.

ABOVE: In 1981, at an informal birthday celebration given by the White House staff, Muffie Brandon presents the first lady with a gift.

OPPOSITE: President and Mrs. Reagan dancing at a White House staff party in December of 1985.

OVERLEAF: The traditional Easter Egg Roll in 1981.

TOP: The children of Washington, D.C., were so angered by legislation that prohibited playing on the Capitol grounds that they stormed the White House gates on the Monday following Easter Day in 1878 demanding entrance. Reportedly, President Rutherford B. Hayes opened the gates and allowed them to enter. The first official Easter Egg Roll on the South Lawn, depicted here in *Frank Leslie's Illustrated Newspaper*, took place that year and the tradition has continued.

BOTTOM: This photo from 1923 shows the annual White House Easter Egg Roll in full swing. The object, as demonstrated by the boys in the photograph, is to roll one's egg as far as possible without cracking it.

OPPOSITE: A delighted guest shows off his basket of Easter treasures.

OVERLEAF: The Easter egg roll of 1981 featured wooded eggs painted and decorated by artists, White House staff, and elected officials including President and Mrs. Reagan and Vice President and Mrs. Bush. Since 1994, each state has sent a decorated egg to the White House for the annual Easter celebration.

The crowd cheers Mrs. Reagan's return to the White House after successful breast cancer surgery on October 22, 1987. The first lady received support not only from the White House staff, but also from well-wishers across the country and around the world. It was a particularly difficult time for the Reagans. The president also had surgery for cancer, Mrs. Reagan's mother, Edith Davis, had died a few months earlier, and the White House was in the midst of the Iran-Contra scandal. The outpouring of affection was uplifting and overwhelming.

ABOVE: A Fourth of July reveler shows off an antique car on the
South Lawn of the White House.

OPPOSITE: A Fourth of July barbecue for White House staff hosted
by President and Mrs. Reagan in appreciation of the staff's long
hours and hard work.

CHAPTER SIX

Matters of State

Matters of State

STATE DINNERS ARE ALL MEMORABLE. BUT THE GALA event hosted for Mikhail Gorbachev on a chilly night in December of 1987 was in many ways the most important and challenging of the Reagan years. Presidents Reagan and Gorbachev had developed a productive relationship that culminated in the first visit by a Soviet leader to Washington since Nikita Khrushchev in 1959. After years of hard work and countless hours of negotiations, the two countries would sign a treaty to eliminate an entire class of nuclear weapons. There was a growing sense that the Cold War, a period of tension and competition that existed between the United States and the Soviet Union from the mid-1940s, could finally end, and that the two leaders who would toast one another at the White House on December 8 were largely responsible.

After the dinner and toasts, famed pianist Van Cliburn played a selection of Brahms and Debussy. As the candles flickered, Cliburn surprised the crowd with a rendition of "Moscow Nights," a traditional Russian ballad that is as emotional to a Russian as "Danny Boy" is to an Irishman. After a few bars, Gorbachev broke into song. By the second verse, every Soviet in the room was singing. In the East Room of the White House, surrounded by Cold War hawks like Jeane Kirkpatrick and Dick Cheney, the leaders of the Communist Party were serenading the guests.

Throughout their years at the White House, President and Mrs. Reagan were honored to host presidents, royalty, and diplomats from around the world. By the time they left office in 1989, the Reagans had given fifty-five state dinners and hundreds of other events, both intimate and grand. "It was a vital part of our roles as president and first lady," recalls Mrs. Reagan. "And it was a duty that we enjoyed immensely."

State dinners are no substitute for skilled negotiations, but they can play a vital role in strengthening the bonds between nations and bolstering America's position in the world. Political rivals can put aside differences and enjoy a cordial, nonpartisan evening. "Formal entertaining at the White House involves something that has almost disappeared in recent years," says columnist George Will, observing, "Democrats and Republicans mingle together."

Life in the White House comes with pressures, but the few months leading up to the Gorbachev state dinner had been especially stressful. President Reagan had been battered by the Iran-Contra scandal. Mrs. Reagan was recovering from surgery for breast cancer, and was still grieving for her mother, who had died less than two months before. Nevertheless, the opportunity presented by the Gorbachevs' visit to the White House was unprecedented. It was a chance to introduce Gorbachev and his wife, Raisa, to some of the country's best and brightest citizens. It was also an opportunity for Mrs. Reagan and Raisa Gorbachev to improve their relationship, as it was no secret that their prior meetings had not resulted in the warmest friendship. More than anything, the dinner would symbolize the thawing of the Cold War and solidify new relations between the two nations.

BY INVITATION ONLY

In an era of informality, state dinners remain one of the last bastions of formal, ceremonial entertaining. The White House tries to make sure that the evening is friendly and enjoyable, but no one pretends that this is a casual dinner party, nor should they. The government pays for the gatherings, but it is the responsibility of the first lady to sign off on the myriad details that ultimately lead to the success or failure of a state dinner, not the least of which is deciding who will attend. In short, the first lady must balance the dictates of protocol with her own artful intuition. "It's her house," observed one White House staffer. "So it's her party."

Given the enormous anticipation of the Gorbachev Summit, the White House was deluged with requests for invitations. This would be the most coveted event since the visit of Princess Diana and Prince Charles in 1985. Early in the administration, Mrs. Reagan and her staff had made the decision to stay with the "magic number" of ninety-six guests for a formal dinner. In this case, however, the various officials involved in planning the event, including the State Department, Mrs. Reagan's office, and the White House social secretary, agreed that it was impossible to adhere to this limit.

Some invitations to a state dinner are required as a matter of protocol, including those to the vice president and his wife, the delegation from the visiting state, congressmen, and various government officials. Friends of the Reagans were often invited. The doctors and nurses who helped President Reagan recover from the 1981 assassination attempt attended several different dinners. The Reagans also once invited John Musante, their longtime grocer in California.

The guest list is also influenced by political and diplomatic rivalries. The White House is acutely aware that a published list of guests is taken as a barometer of who is in favor and who is out. It is good to know who deserves to be rewarded for good work and whom the administration would be working closely with in the future. In the case of the Gorbachev dinner, it was important to know whom the Soviets would like to be on hand and who could speak fluent Russian to make the foreign delegation feel welcome.

With few discretionary invitations left, lobbying among potential guests was intense. One woman went too far by contacting various officials at different times, very much like a congressman lobbying for a bill. The usual shyness in such matters dissolves during the approach of a historic state dinner. "People tried everything," recalls Social Secretary Gahl Hodges Burt. "It would take your breath away."

White House social secretaries collect names and subscribe to dozens of magazines in search of "bright lights" to fill the East Room. In the Reagan years, a rack in the social secretary's office contained marked folders for different categories of notable people, such as "Clergy," "Minorities," "Personalities," "Actors," "Single Men," and "Single Women." Into each folder would go relevant clippings or notes taken while watching *Good Morning America* or nightly televised news.

"My husband and I always tried to assemble a group who would do honor to the country," remembers Mrs. Reagan.

By the time Mrs. Reagan and her staff had finalized the guest list in November of 1987, dozens of officials had entered into preparation plans. Two different offices in the State Department checked the list, as did the National Security Council and at least five offices in the West Wing of the White House. A call to presidential advisors Ed Rollins and Lee Atwater would usually result in a warning that "We've got to get to congressman so-and-so, so get him on the list," recalls Hodges Burt. A tentative list would be sent to the offices of top presidential advisors Mike Deaver, Ed Meese, and James Baker. The high-powered "troika," as they were called, would refine the list further, either adding or crossing out names. In the

end, however, it was the first lady and her advisors who made the decision.

An invitation to the White House does not carry the weight of a royal command. Given the honor of the invitation, there are very few excuses apart from illness or a death in the family that pass muster. Some observances of etiquette have been put aside. The formality of a written response has faded into history. A phone call to the social secretary is acceptable. A guest can also bring anyone he or she chooses, not just a spouse or a grown child—provided, of course, that the guest is not a security risk.

For the Gorbachev dinner, many of the uninvited lobbied for inclusion, and if unsuccessful, made excuses to friends as to why they could not attend. Some in high society make travel plans and leave town to provide cover for a lack of a White House invitation. "I have to be in Tokyo that week," one socialite is reported to have said.

The frenzy was understandable. The Gorbachev State Dinner would put guests in the front row of history with the added pleasure of a fine meal.

Countless other details needed to be resolved, including menus, floral arrangements, security issues, and entertainment. Social Secretary Linda Faulkner had the inspired idea of asking renowned pianist Van Cliburn to perform. The pianist had arrived on the world stage in 1958 when he became the first American to win the Tchaikovsky Competition in Moscow. Still revered by Russians, his presence would delight the Soviet delegation and send a clear message of goodwill. The gravity and grandeur of the event convinced the legendary musician to give his first live performance in nine years. "It was a perfect fit," recalls Mrs. Reagan.

Months before his White House performance, a Russian pianist known for his startling psychic abilities had told Cliburn, "I think the next time you play, it will have something to do with Russia." When the White House called and asked him to interrupt his sabbatical for the sake of world peace, Cliburn recalled the premonition, but would have shown up in any case. "It is always a great honor to play in the East Room," says Cliburn. "I love the acoustics and the warmth. I love its sense of history."

IN FROM THE COLD

The goal of any state dinner is to offer guests a front row view of America's brilliance and diversity. World leaders, given a few hours to share a global stage with the president, expect nothing less, and so it was for the Gorbachev dinner.

In the moments before the guests arrived, butlers and military

ABOVE: State dinners offer a pleasant break for officials who have spent the day hashing out summit details. Here, Colin Powell greets Raisa Gorbachev in the reception line in 1987. "Invariably, we'd be crashing an hour before the state dinner to get our work done," recalls Powell, then President Reagan's national security advisor. "Once we were at the dinner, we tried to keep it as a social event. That's not to say that corner conversations wouldn't discuss what happened that day. But we tried to keep it relaxed."

RIGHT: Original White House invitations to the USSR state dinner.

PAGE 162: The U.S. Army Old Guard Fife and Drum Corps, whose origins date back to the musicians of the Continental Army of George Washington, reassembles during the arrival of Venezuelan President Luis Herrera Campins in 1981. President and Mrs. Reagan restored the ceremonial use of the group to bolster the arrival of visiting dignitaries.

PAGE 164: President and Mrs. Reagan pose with President and Mrs. Gorbachev outside the White House prior to the state dinner.

The President and Mrs. Reagan
request the pleasure of the company of

at dinner
on Tuesday, December 8, 1987
at 6:45 o'clock

Black Tie

On the occasion of the visit of
His Excellency
The General Secretary of the Central Committee
of the Communist Party of the Soviet Union
and Mrs. Gorbachev

LEFT: In the interval between dinner and dessert, members of the U.S. Air Force Strolling Strings serenade the crowd. President Dwight Eisenhower introduced the idea of this musical interlude to the White House in 1957 for a state dinner honoring the king of Saudi Arabia. The Strolling Strings have become an elegant mainstay of White House entertaining. "It was always one of my favorite moments," recalls Mrs. Reagan.

BELOW: The menu at the Gorbachev dinner did not attempt to replicate Russian cuisine. It did, however, feature a caviar sauce as a culinary nod to the Soviet Union. The champagne used for toasts, an Iron Horse Brut, was bottled near the Russian River, an area of Russian settlement in the 1800s. The symbolism was not lost on the Soviet delegation, who regarded the selection as a sign of respect.

DINNER
Honoring
His Excellency
The General Secretary of the Central Committee
of the Communist Party of the Soviet Union
and Mrs. Gorbachev

Columbia River Salmon &
Lobster Medallions en Gelée
Caviar Sauce
Fennel Seed Twists

Loin of Veal with Wild Mushrooms
Champagne Sauce
Tarragon Tomatoes
Corn Turban

Medley of Garden Greens,
Brie Cheese with Crushed Walnuts
Vinegar & Avocado Oil Dressing

Tea Sorbet in Honey Ice Cream

JORDAN *Chardonnay* 1984
STAGS' LEAP *Cabernet-Sauvignon Lot 2* 1978
IRON HORSE *Brut Summit Cuvée* 1984

THE WHITE HOUSE
Tuesday, December 8, 1987

Richard Perle, assistant secretary of defense, sitting at Mrs. Reagan's left, asked Gorbachev pointed questions about the Soviet military and the Politburo. When Perle asked a question about the percentage of the Soviet budget dedicated to the military, Gorbachev balked. "I won't answer that," he said brusquely. Still, the Soviet leader seemed to enjoy the spirit of their conversation. Unlike some foreign leaders, Gorbachev liked being challenged.

aides stood ready in the corridors and throughout the public rooms. The lights were lowered. A group of extra workers began assembling the dishes in the Family Dining Room, now used mostly as a staging area for the State Dining Room. A line of limousines approached the East Gate of the White House at 6:30. The weather was frigid, but the public rooms of the White House were warm and elegant. Under the artful eye of Mrs. Reagan's interior designer, Ted Graber, the "People's House" was decorated with ferns, holly, and lilies. The guests were greeted by harp and flute music as they made their way through the East Wing corridors and then, guided by social aides, into the East Room.

Among the celebrities who arrived that evening was baseball legend Joe DiMaggio, who brought a baseball and asked both President Reagan and President Gorbachev to sign it. "I always wondered what happened to that ball," says Mrs. Reagan. "What a collector's item it must be." Other guests included movie veteran Jimmy Stewart, Olympic gymnast Mary Lou Retton, evangelist Billy Graham, singer Pearl Bailey, actress Claudette Colbert, author Saul Bellow, musician Dave Brubeck, conductor Zubin Mehta, and oil industrialist Armand Hammer.

Upstairs, President and Mrs. Reagan greeted the Gorbachevs and a few other guests for a quiet cocktail in the Yellow Room of the private quarters. Then, as the Marine Band played "Hail to the Chief," the president and first lady escorted the Gorbachevs down the Grand Staircase into the East Room.

All state dinners are black tie affairs. White tie is used only for royalty, not heads of government. President Reagan was in a black tuxedo, but Gorbachev wore a three-piece blue suit, then still a rarity in Russia. The Soviet president had to consider perceptions back home, where a capitalist tuxedo would be considered too bourgeois. President Anwar Sadat of Egypt had similar concerns, as did guests from China, who also wore suits.

Mrs. Reagan wore a black beaded gown by James Galanos, one of her favorite designers. It was embellished with red and white flowers, and a bow at the waist. Raisa Gorbachev wore a beautiful black brocade gown and a double strand of pearls.

The Gorbachevs had done their homework. In the East Room reception line, they knew something about each guest who shook their hands. Small talk ensued. This was wonderful for visitors, of course, who each had a conversation with the Reagans and Gorbachevs, but the slow pace became a problem for Mrs. Reagan; the timing of the dinner had been carefully planned, especially since the Soviet delegation had insisted on an early evening.

Protocol dictates that the president, first lady, and honored guests sit down at their tables before other guests. "Such honors were in recognition of the office, not the office holder," remembers Mrs. Reagan.

AT TABLE

In the days leading up to state dinners, Mrs. Reagan and her staff pored over seating charts to come up with a lively but noncombative mix of guests at each of the thirteen tables that would be gathered in the State Dining Room. In anticipation of last-minute additions and subtractions to the guest list, Mrs. Reagan and her staff would usually wait until the morning of the dinner to finalize seating as, inevitably, some guests simply fail to show up. To simplify this process, they placed a square board with thirteen round circles on the floor of Mrs. Reagan's study. The circles represented the tables, and the white slips of paper used to represent each guest could be easily moved for placement.

"Mrs. Reagan had a magic touch in seating people next to one another," recalls Social Secretary Gahl Hodges Burt. "More than once, she said to me, 'Oh Gahl, you can't put those two next to each other.' I felt dumb, but how could I have known? I learned."

It was no accident, for example, that Jeane Kirkpatrick, then the U.S. ambassador to the United Nations, was seated next to President Reagan. Kirkpatrick was a staunch foe of the arms treaty, but here she was at the president's elbow. It was a visible sign of the country's unity. She would also be of great interest to the Soviets, who seemed far more interested in their opponents than their supporters.

Across the State Dining Room, Secretary of State George Shultz shared the table with Marshal Sergei Akhromeyev, his counterpart in the Soviet Union. "I was a sergeant during the siege of Leningrad," Akhromeyev told Schultz. "I felt like I served my country. I haven't felt that same sense of pride until now." Stunned by Akhromeyev's emotional analogy to the historic battle against the Nazis, Schultz considered it a clear indication that the dinner had been a huge success. "It is not the kind of thing a person would say at a formal meeting," Schultz observes.

BREAKING BREAD

After much consideration, Mrs. Reagan decided on a first course of Columbia River salmon with lobster medallions in caviar sauce, followed by a loin of veal with wild mushrooms in champagne sauce, with zucchini boats filled with vegetables. Dessert was honey ice cream with petits fours.

The menu at this state dinner would honor the guest coun-

try without trying to replicate its cuisine. It would have been poor taste, for example, to serve beef stroganoff to Soviet guests. But it made perfect sense to refer to their cuisine by serving a caviar sauce with the first course.

Most foreign delegations will inform the protocol office of any special dietary requirements. The Soviets claimed that they liked just about everything. This may simply have been good manners, but they may also have been wary of providing personal details that could later be used in intelligence gathering. The Cold War was ending, but it wasn't over yet.

President and Mrs. Reagan were partial to wines of their home state of California. For toasts at the Gorbachev dinner, they served a 1984 Iron Horse brut, a sparkling wine that had been used during the Reagan-Gorbachev summit in Geneva. The wine was bottled near the Russian River, an area of Russian settlement in the 1800s.

Guests to state dinners sometimes help themselves to small souvenirs such as matchbooks or menus that can be auto-

graphed by other guests. In earlier days, a large number of silver forks and knives and even small plates typically went missing after state dinners. "It's probably still happening today," Mrs. Reagan jokes.

A LITTLE NIGHT MUSIC

The Reagans hosted hundreds of great performers at the White House, from Frank Sinatra to Itzahk Perlman. None, however, were more memorable than Van Cliburn. His performance of a Brahms intermezzo and a short piece by Rachmaninoff was met with thunderous applause, especially from President Gorbachev, who hugged and kissed the pianist. "It is a pity you don't have an orchestra and you could play Tchaikovsky," Raisa Gorbachev teased. Cliburn replied that there was one encore he could offer. He then returned to his piano to perform the emotional rendition of "Moscow Nights." The ensuing sing-along among the Soviets ended a memorable night on a most memorable note.

The hard work of the staff and many offices throughout Washington had paid off. "I think everyone felt a great sense of privilege," said the late J. Carter Brown, then head of the National Gallery of Art. "And that gives an evening a kind of electricity."

Both presidents offered eloquent toasts about the prospects for peace between nations. "So I offer a toast," said President Reagan. "A commitment on behalf of the American people of seriousness, goodwill, and hope for the future."

"Winter," said Gorbachev on that cold December night, "is on the wane."

"It was a perfect ending," concludes Mrs. Reagan, "for one of the great evenings of my husband's presidency."

ABOVE AND OPPOSITE: After the final chord of Debussy's *L'Isle Joyeuse*, the Reagans and Gorbachevs rushed to the stage to embrace pianist Van Cliburn. "I wish you could play something else," Raisa Gorbachev said. Cliburn remembered a song he had learned in 1958 during his triumphant visit to Russia. "Moscow Nights" had become a kind of national anthem. He had not played the piece in years, but when he sat down in the East Room, it all came back. "The mood of the evening had shifted," he recalls. "It had become less formal and more intimate."

The two superpower leaders toast a successful, historic summit. "Winter," Gorbachev observed, "is on the wane."

"President Gorbachev and my husband had a certain chemistry that helped improve relations," recalls Mrs. Reagan. "Their friendship continued even after both had left office."

"We felt the ice of the Cold War crumbling."

—GEORGE SHULTZ, Former Secretary of State
on Gorbachev's 1987 state visit

"A state dinner is the highest social honor we can bestow on another country. It is very much sought after. If we've honored a country with a state dinner, it means that that country is certainly in good standing with the United States."

—COLIN POWELL, Former Secretary of State

President and Mrs. Reagan share a laugh with Bob Hope during the first state dinner for Prime Minister Margaret Thatcher in 1981. Hope was invited because of both his friendship with the president and his British roots.

Clint Eastwood greets Prime Minister Yasuhiro Nakasone of
Japan in 1981 as Douglas Fairbanks Jr. looks on. Film celebrities
have been invited to state dinners since the early days of
Hollywood.

RIGHT: Mrs. Reagan talks with the wife of Chancellor Helmut Kohl, Hannelore Kohl, during a 1982 dinner honoring the German leader.

OPPOSITE TOP: Mrs. Reagan escorts President Anwar Sadat into the East Room in 1981. This would be Sadat's final visit to the White House; he was assassinated in Egypt less than two months later.

OPPOSITE BOTTOM LEFT: State dinners usually include more men than women, largely because of the delegation from the visiting country. Mrs. Reagan disliked the imbalance and would often invite single women to equalize the table seatings. Vanessa Williams, the newly crowned Miss America, arrives at the 1983 state dinner for Chancellor Karl Carstens of West Germany. Nancy Reagan initiated sending military aides to escort single women to the White House.

OPPOSITE BOTTOM RIGHT: Sally Danforth looks on as Nancy Reagan chats with the Sultan of Oman in 1983.

Mrs. Reagan at table with President Anwar Sadat of Egypt in 1981.

LEFT TOP: Mrs. Reagan in 1983 with King Birendra of Nepal.

LEFT BOTTOM: How food should arrive to the table has evolved over the years. Thomas Jefferson set up trays from which guests served themselves. Other first ladies have opted to have a prepared plate of food delivered to each guest. Mrs. Reagan chose French service, in which guests serve themselves from a tray, and here serves herself dessert as Prime Minister Yasuhiro Nakasone of Japan looks on.

ABOVE: At age seventy-two, legendary musician Benny Goodman leads a jazz quintet in his first performance at the White House. Frank Sinatra, who arranged much of the entertainment during the Reagan administration, enlisted Goodman for the state dinner honoring King Hussein of Jordan. Buddy Rich, Goodman's drummer for the evening, said that Sinatra jokingly asked him "to stop off here."

OPPOSITE: Secretary of State George Shultz lives out a boyhood fantasy by playing Fred Astaire to Ginger Rogers. "I recall that at the table, she wanted to talk about foreign policy," says Shultz. "And I wanted to talk about dancing." For someone so renowned in government, Shultz was considered a graceful dancer. Apparently Rogers agreed. "Dear George," she signed on a copy of this photo, "What fun. For the first few moments, I thought I was dancing with Fred."

ABOVE: The first dance at a state dinner for British Prime Minister Margaret Thatcher.

RIGHT: King Juan Carlos of Spain invites Mrs. Reagan to the dance floor.

OVERLEAF: President Reagan shares the stage with Ella Fitzgerald in 1981.

LEFT: Frank Sinatra had little time to rehearse for this 1984 performance at the state dinner for Sri Lanka. Because of the bombing of the marine barracks in Beirut eight months earlier, tightened security required everything, including musical instruments, to be sniffed by dogs for explosives. The burden placed on the animals during state visits was enormous. On the day of Sinatra's show, the overworked dogs became too exhausted to perform their duty, leaving Sinatra's instruments stranded outside the East Gate. Sinatra had to wait while replacement dogs were brought in from another military installation. From that day forward, there was a fresh team of dogs on hand before each state dinner.

OPPOSITE: In 1982 Frank Sinatra and Perry Como relax after a performance at the state dinner for Alessandro Pertini, the prime minister of Italy. The White House tries to form a connection or theme between the guest and the entertainment. On this night, they enlisted the two great singers of Italian heritage.

President John Kennedy chats with author Pearl Buck in 1962 as First Lady Jacqueline Kennedy listens to poet laureate Robert Frost. Occasionally, help is needed in the East Room; during performances, social secretary Letitia Baldrige would open a nearby door slightly to signal to the president that it was time to applaud.

A performance of Twyla Tharp's "Nine Sinatra Songs" for the 1984 state dinner for Luxembourg posed several challenges. Dancers were concerned that some of the leaps from a riser would take them straight into a historic chandelier. The solution? Dance on the floor. Mrs. Reagan suggested that floor risers be built around the dancers, and small tables set up with small chairs and candles, for a more intimate atmosphere. White House staffers were also concerned that the dance might be a bit risqué for the East Room under the gaze of George and Martha Washington's portraits. According to a White House staffer, Tharp bristled at suggestions of toning down the dance. But she solved the problem by costuming the dancers in leotards. Mrs. Reagan said the performance was "magical."

LEFT: President and Mrs. Reagan congratulate Sarah Vaughn after her performance at the 1987 dinner for the nation's governors. When Vaughn entertained for a state dinner during the Johnson administration, White House social secretary Bess Abell found her in her dressing room crying. "Nothing's the matter," she said through tears. "It's just that twenty years ago when I came to Washington, I couldn't even get a hotel room, and tonight I sang for the president of the United States in the White House–and he asked me to dance. It's more than I can stand."

OPPOSITE TOP: Itzhak Perlman performs for President Hosni Mubarak of Egypt in 1982. In an important symbolic gesture, the White House asked an Israeli musician to perform for the Egyptian delegation.

OPPOSITE BOTTOM: Violinist Isaac Stern, left, is praised by Premier Zhao Ziyang of the People's Republic of China in 1984. Earlier, Stern had caused a panic by going missing just as guests were filing into the East Room for his performance. Social secretary Gahl Hodges Burt, who struggled through difficult negotiations with Stern's publicist, began to wonder if the famed musician was also temperamental, as he was missing. As the Marine Band started to play, she looked down into the orchestra and was relieved to see the great violinist, playing along happily as just another member of the band. "The faces on those Marines were incredible," recalls Hodges Burt. "They were so proud." Later, Stern stayed behind to sign a piece of sheet music for every band member.

President and Mrs. Reagan finish the night with a dance after the state dinner for King Juan Carlos of Spain. Guests at state dinners usually stayed for a short while after the president and first lady departed. "I couldn't keep Ronnie up past eleven fifteen," Mrs. Reagan jokes.

White House State Dinners

REAGAN ADMINISTRATION

The Right Honorable
Margaret Thatcher, M.P.
Prime Minister of the United Kingdom of
Great Britain and Northern Ireland
and Mr. Thatcher

February 26, 1981

His Excellency
The Prime Minister of Japan
and Mrs. Suzuki

May 7, 1981

His Excellency
The Chancellor of the
Federal Republic of Germany
and Mrs. Schmidt

May 21, 1981

The Right Honorable
The Prime Minister of Australia
and Mrs. Fraser

June 30, 1981

His Excellency
The President of the
Arab Republic of Egypt
and Mrs. Sadat

August 5, 1981

His Excellency
Menachem Begin
Prime Minister of Israel

September 9, 1981

Their Majesties
The King and Queen of Spain

October 13, 1981

Their Majesties
The King and Queen
of the Hashemite Kingdom of Jordan

November 2, 1981

His Excellency
The President of the Republic of Venezuela
and Mrs. Campins

November 17, 1981

His Excellency
The President of the Arab Republic of Egypt
and Mrs. Mubarak

February 3, 1982

His Excellency
Sandro Pertini
President of the Italian Republic

March 25, 1982

Her Majesty the Queen
and His Royal Highness Prince Claus
of the Netherlands

April 19, 1982

His Excellency
The President of the
Federative Republic of Brazil
and Mrs. Figueiredo

May 12, 1982

Her Excellency Indira Gandhi
Prime Minister of India

July 29, 1982

His Excellency
The President of the Republic
of the Philippines
& Mrs. Marcos

September 16, 1982

His Excellency
The President of the Republic
of Indonesia
and Mrs. Soeharto
October 12, 1982

His Excellency
The President of the Islamic Republic
of Pakistan
and Begum Zia-ul-Haq
December 7, 1982

His Majesty
Sultan Qaboos bin Said
Sultan of Oman
April 12, 1983

His Excellency
The President of the
Republic of Ivory Coast
and Madame Houphouet-Boigny
June 7, 1983

His Highness
Shaikh Isa bin Salman
Al-Khalifa
Amir of the State of Bahrain
July 19, 1983

His Excellency
The President of the
Republic of Portugal
and Dr. Maria Manuela Eanes
September 15, 1983

His Excellency
The President of the
Federal Republic of Germany
and Mrs. Carstens
October 4, 1983

Their Majesties
The King and Queen
of Nepal
December 7, 1983

His Excellency
The Premier of the State Council
of the People's Republic of China
January 10, 1984

His Excellency,
The President of the Republic of Austria
and Mrs. Kirchschlaeger
February 28, 1984

His Excellency
The President of the French Republic
and Mrs. Mitterand
March 22, 1984

His Excellency
The President of the Dominican Republic
and Mrs. Jorge Blanco
April 10, 1984

His Excellency
The President of Mexico
and Mrs. de la Madrid
May 15, 1984

His Excellency
The President of the Democratic Socialist Republic
of Sri Lanka
and Mrs. Jayewardene
June 18, 1984

Their Royal Highnesses
The Grand Duke and the Grand Duchess
of Luxembourg
November 13, 1984

His Excellency
Dr. Jaime Lusinchi
President of the Republic of Venezuela
December 4, 1984

His Majesty
Fahd ibn Abd al-Aziz Al Saud
King of Saudi Arabia
February 11, 1985

His Excellency
The President of the Argentine Republic
and Mrs. Alfonsin
March 19, 1985

His Excellency
The President of the Democratic and
Popular Republic of Algeria
and Mrs. Bendjedid
April 17, 1985

His Excellency
The Prime Minister of India
and Mrs. Gandhi
June 12, 1985

His Excellency
The President of the Peoples Republic of China
and Madame Lin Jedmei
July 23, 1985

His Excellency
The Prime Minister of Denmark
and Mrs. Schlueter
September 10, 1985

His Excellency
The Prime Minister of the Republic of Singapore
and Mrs. Lee
October 8, 1985

His Excellency
The President of the Republic of Ecuador
and Mrs. Febres-Cordero
January 14, 1986

His Excellency
The President of the
Federative Republic of Brazil
and Mrs. Sarney

September 10, 1986

His Excellency
The Chancellor of the Federal Republic of Germany
and Mrs. Kohl

October 21, 1986

His Excellency
The Prime Minister of the
French Republic
and Mrs. Chirac

October 21, 1986

His Excellency
The President of the Republic of El Salvador
and Mrs. Duarte
Wednesday, October 14, 1987

His Excellency
The President of Israel
and Mrs. Herzog

November 10, 1987

His Excellency
The General Secretary of the Central Committee
of the Communist Party of the Soviet Union
and Mrs. Gorbachev

December 8, 1987

His Excellency
The President
of the Arab Republic of Egypt
and Mrs. Mubarak

January 28, 1988

Honoring
The Right Honorable
The Prime Minister of Canada
and Mrs. Mulroney
Wednesday, April 27, 1988

His Excellency Kenan Evren

President of the Republic of Turkey

June 27, 1988

His Excellency
The President
of the Republic of Mali
and
Mrs. Traore
October 6, 1988

The Right Honorable
The Prime Minister of the United Kingdom
of
Great Britain and Northern Ireland
and
Mr. Thatcher

November 16, 1988

Epilogue

FROM PRESIDENT REAGAN'S DIARIES

"The State Dinner was a success. I'm encouraged that between us maybe we can do something about peace in the Middle East." [1]

"The State Dinner was a smash from 1st cocktail to the last dance… I believe we've really established a bond of friendship. His Majesty's response to the toast was obviously sincere, warm & moving." [2]

"It was a warm & pleasant affair… His remarks at dinner were very humorous. We made a friend." [3]

"Everyone seemed to have fun. His Majesty is a really shy man & I'm convinced he felt he had been befriended. I invited him to come to the W.H. for breakfast." [4]

"It (again) was a most enjoyable evening. I give Nancy credit. I've been to state dinners before I had this job & they were stuffy, impersonal & dull. Our state dinners are enjoyable, everyone has fun & the guest list is always an interesting mix." [5]

1. August 5,1981 President Anwar Sadat, Egypt, p. 35
2. November 2, 1981 King Ali bin Hussein, Jordan, p. 47
3. July 19, 1983 Shaikh Isa bin Salman Al-Khalifa, Bahrain, p. 167
4. February 11, 1985 King Fahd ibn Abd al-Aziz Al Saud, Saudi Arabia, p. 300
5. March 18, 1986 Prime Minister Brian Mulroney, Canada, p. 399

Reagan, Ronald. The Reagan Diaries. New York: HarperCollins, 2007.

Acknowledgments

WE ARE GRATEFUL TO THE MANY FRIENDS AND colleagues throughout the country whose support for this book is a tribute to President and Mrs. Reagan. Jean Hayden Mathison provided photographs from the Ted Graber collection, and her enthusiasm and respect for the White House inspired us to begin this project.

She also introduced us to our agent, Michael Hamilburg, who submitted the idea to HarperCollins. Anna Bliss and Richard Ljoenes of HarperCollins were very helpful and patient as we worked through deadlines. Stafford Cliff's keen eye for design guided our initial concept of the book, and Stephen Schmidt followed through with an able and inspired hand. Dirk Mathison's dedicated research and enthusiasm was greatly appreciated. He conducted all interviews included in this book with expert flair.

The busy staff of the White House were very helpful. Gary J. Walters, the former chief usher of the White House, conducted a lengthy tour of the People's House and offered insight into the inner workings of the executive mansion, and Nancy Clarke, the White House florist, guided us through a typical day of arranging flowers for the entire house. George Shultz, Colin Powell, Ambassador Robert Tuttle, Fred Ryan, and Carolyn and Mike Deaver shared stories about their days in the White House.

The able staff of the Ronald Reagan Presidential Library helped us to access the myriad documents and photographs of the Reagan years. Ray Wilson and Steve Branch at the library's audiovisual department worked tirelessly to provide the photographs.

Joanne Drake, Wren Powell, and Kirby Hanson were very helpful at the library and helped to coordinate interviews across the country, including at the White House.

The White House Historical Association generously provided dozens of photographs and Hilary Crehan was ever cordial as we requested additional images. The Library of Congress supplied us images from their historic collection of early photographs which were an invaluable contribution to this book.

Catherine Allgor, George Will, and William Seale offered brilliant insight into the history of presidential entertaining. Van Cliburn called from Texas to relate stories about his celebrated appearance in the East Room. Betsy Bloomingdale, Jon Musante, and David Jones talked about their days with their friends.

Selwa Roosevelt and Leonore Annenberg explained the world of protocol. Letitia Baldrige, Linda Faulkner, and Gahl Hodges Burt offered stories from the unique perspective of the White House Social Secretary's office.

Finally, we would like to thank our friend Nancy Reagan who shared her scrapbooks, fed us cookies, and remained cheerful and supportive for the duration of the project.

NOTES

CHAPTER 1: 1801

3 "few people in this world": John Adams to Abigail Adams, August 18, 1776, *Adams Family Papers: An Electronic Archive*. Massachusetts Historical Society. http://www.masshist.org/digitaladams/.

3 "moving only in an official": Devens, *Pictorial Anecdotes*, 645.

3 "Washington was dealing": Will/Mathison interview.

4 "And those were long dinners": Will/Mathison interview.

4 "I could not get relieved": Marshall, *The Life of George Washington*, 145.

4 "We are informed": Seale, *The President's House*, 5.

4 "Mr. Jefferson mingled": Smith, *First Forty Years*, 30.

4 "rigorously frugal and simple": Jefferson to Elbridge Gerry, January 26, 1799, *The Jeffersonian Cyclopedia: A Comprehensive Collection of the Views of Thomas Jefferson*, 272.

7 "Many people . . . made appointments": Whitcomb, *Real Life at the White House*, 27.

7 "It was impossible": Allgor, *Parlor Politics*, 77.

7 "Dolly combined sumptuous settings": Allgor, *Actors and Observers*, 25.

CHAPTER 1: CAPTIONS

5 "Shiver, shiver": Singleton, *Story of the White House*, 13.

6 "But in her hands": Ibid., 71.

8 "more and more insupportable": Adams, *Memoirs of John Quincy Adams*, Feb. 20, 1828.

8 "a hard time of it": Whitcomb, *Real Life at the White House*, 51.

8 "Not a whisper": Ibid., 43.

9 "The great wood-fires": Singleton, *Story of the White House*, 213.

10 "It has always been a challenge": Seale/Mathison interview.

11 "So glad to see you.": Seale, *The President's House*, 607.

14 "I must go to dinner": Nevins, *Cleveland: A Study in Courage*, 212.

15 "My first public appearance": Whitcomb, citing Edith Wilson, *My Memoir*, 1939, in *Real Life at the White House*, 254.

15 "scrambled eggs with brains": West, *Upstairs at the White House*, 20.

16 "God set up the barrier": Manis, *Macon Black and White*, 3.

17 "swollen like a poisoned pup": Seale, *The President's House*, 406.

18 "Cut glass and china": Smith, *First Forty Years*, 295–296.

38 "I took a step": Seale, *The President's House*, 607.

CHAPTER 2: ETIQUETTE AND PROTOCOL

43 "from design and not from ignorance": Anthony Merry to British foreign officer George R. Hammond, Dec., 7, 1803, Allgor, *Parlor Politics*.

43 "respected and welcome": Annenberg/Mathison interview.

43 "President Reagan once told me": Roosevelt/Mathison interview.

43 "You can't believe": Roosevelt/Mathison interview.

44 "Does not like rare roast beef": Memo from office of White House social secretary, collection of Ronald Reagan Library, Feb. 26, 1981.

CHAPTER 2: CAPTIONS

51 "I wish they would": Carpenter, *The Inner Life of Abraham Lincoln*, 143.

58 "I think this is the most extraordinary": http//www.presidency.ucsb.edu/ws/print.php?pid=8623.

58 "He put his arm": Kirk, *Music at the White House*, 180.

62 "In the Reagan White House": Mike Deaver/Mathison interview.

67 "The press would just tear it up": Walters/Mathison interview.

67 "Sure, let's do it": Powell/Mathison interview.

CHAPTER 3: ELEMENTS OF STYLE

73 "This is the President's House": Ryan/Mathison interview.

73 "Everything you do": Mensier, White House website, July 7, 2004: http://www.whitehouse.gov/ask/20040727.html.

73 "The table was large": Cooper, *Notions of the Americans*, 54–55.

73 "a piece of cornbread": Whitcomb, *Real Life at the White House*, 97.

73 "My social secretary": Ibid., 417.

73 "the water flowed like champagne": Boller, *Anecdotes*, 165.

74 "a dinner without wine": Barnard, *Rutherford B. Hayes, and His America*, 480.

74 "Bird, let's have Congress": Whitcomb, *Real Life at the White House*, 378, citing Whalen, *The Longest Debate: A Legislative History of the 1964 Civil Rights Act*.

74 "Everything is just so easy": Baldrige/Mathison interview.

74 "She expected the highest quality": Walters/Mathison interview.

74 "The Reagan parties were always very elegant": Powell/Mathison interview.

CHAPTER 3: CAPTIONS

75 "Once in a while": Whitcomb, 155.

81 "It is a very specific shade": Carder/Mathison interview.

85 "The White House staff was wonderful": Jones/Mathison interview.

85 "When she left the White House": Clarke/Mathison interview.

85 "We have such a range of colors": Clarke/Mathison interview.

95 "We've done a lot better": Burros, *New York Times*, June 7, 1987.

95 "Menus are based": Walters/Mathison interview.

CHAPTER 4: PRIVATE GATHERINGS

105 "These kind of parties": Walters/Mathison interview.

105 "scrambled eggs with brains": West, *Upstairs at the White House*, 20.

106 "Do you think there might be": Deaver/Mathison interview.

106 "President Reagan had a preternatural affability": Will/Mathison interview.

106 "It didn't make a bit of difference": Deaver/Mathison interview.

121 "Those Californians": Bloomingdale/Mathison interview.

122 "He was exactly what you'd hope": Faulkner/Mathison interview.

CHAPTER 5: CELEBRATIONS

132 "It was nerve-racking": Walters/Mathison interview.

132 "You won't believe this": *Los Angeles Times*, Dec. 12, 1988.

132 "with pomp and parades": *Familiar Letters of John Adams and His Wife Abigail Adams*, 194.

CHAPTER 6: MATTERS OF STATE

165 "Democrats and Republicans mingle together": Will/Mathison interview.

166 "People tried everything": Hodges Burt/Mathison interview.

166 "We've got to get to congressman so-and-so": Ibid.

166 "I think the next time you play": Cliburn/Mathison interview.

166 "It's always a great honor": Ibid.

171 "Mrs. Reagan had a magic touch": Hodges Burt/Mathison interview.

171 "I was a sergeant": Shultz/Mathison interview.

171 "It's not the kind of thing": Ibid.

172 "It is a pity": Cliburn/Mathison interview.

173 "a great sense of privilege": Williams, Jeannie. *USA Today*, Dec. 9, 1987.

CHAPTER 6: CAPTIONS

167 "Invariably, we'd be crashing": Powell/Mathison interview.

170 "I won't answer that": Reagan, Nancy, *My Turn*, 350.

173 "The mood of the evening had shifted": Cliburn/Mathison interview.

177 "A state dinner is the highest social honor": Powell/Mathison interview.

184 Sinatra jokingly asked: Gamarekian, *New York Times*, Nov. 3, 1981.

184 "I recall that at the table": Shultz/Mathison interview.

194 "Nothing's the matter": Whitcomb, citing Carpenter, *Ruffles and Flourishes*, 209.

194 "The faces on those Marines": Hodges Burt/Mathison interview.

SELECTED BIBLIOGRAPHY

Adams, John. *Familiar Letters of John Adams and His Wife Abigail Adams.* New York: Hurd and Houghton, 1876.

Adams, John Quincy. *The Memoirs of John Quincy Adams.* J.B. Lippincott & Co., 1874.

Aikman, Lonnelle. *The Living White House.* 10th ed. Washington, D.C.: White House Historical Association, 1996.

Allgor, Catherine. *Parlor Politics: In Which the Ladies of Washington Help Build a City and a Government.* Charlottesville: University Press of Virginia, 2000.

———. *A Perfect Union: Dolley Madison and the Creation of the American Nation.* New York: Henry Holt and Company, 2006.

Baldrige, Letitia. *Of Diamonds and Diplomats.* Boston: Houghton Mifflin Company, 1968.

Barnard, Harry. *Rutherford B. Hayes and His America.* New York: Bobbs-Merrill, 1954.

Boller, Paul F. *Presidential Anecdotes.* Rev. ed. New York: Oxford University Press, 1996.

Burros, Marian. "De Gustibus: A Peek Inside the First Kitchen." *New York Times,* July 5, 1989.

———. "White House Chef to Leave in Fall." *New York Times,* June 7, 1987.

Carpenter, Francis Bicknell. *The Inner Life of Abraham Lincoln: Six Months at the White House.* New York: Hurd and Houghton, 1872.

Clines, Francis X. "The British Have Landed and Washington Is Taken." *New York Times,* November 10, 1985.

Colacello, Bob. *Ronnie & Nancy: Their Path to the White House—1911 to 1980.* New York: Warner Books, 2004.

Cooper, James Fenimore. *Notions of the Americans: Picked Up by a Travelling Bachelor.* Philadelphia: Carey, Lea & Carey, 1832.

Cuniberti, Betty. "Gorbachevs Jar Social Agenda." *Los Angeles Times,* December 7, 1987.

———. "Nancy Reagan Unrolling the Red Carpet." *Los Angeles Times,* November 19, 1987.

———. "The Washington Summit Solemn Toasts Follow State Dinner; Basic Blue Suits." *Los Angeles Times,* December 9, 1987.

DeGregorio, William A. *The Complete Book of U.S. Presidents.* 4th ed. New York: Barricade Books, 1993.

Devens, Richard Miller. *The Pictorial Book of Anecdotes and Incidents of the War of the Rebellion, Civil, Military, Naval and Domestic.* Hartford, Conn.: Hartford Publishing Co., 1866.

Dowd, Maureen. "A Very Special Relationship." *New York Times,* May 7, 1986.

Eaton, William J. "Gorbachev Hosts a Lavish Dinner, Toasts: 'Until We Meet in Moscow.' " *Los Angeles Times,* December 10, 1987.

Edwards, Anne. *The Reagans: Portrait of a Marriage.* New York: St. Martin's Press, 2003.

"Farewell to Nancy." *Los Angeles Times,* August 18, 1988.

Gamarekian, Barbara. "All the President's Popcorn." *New York Times,* May 23, 1985.

———. "A Santa of Sorts Joins White House Tour." *New York Times,* December 10, 1985.

———. "A State Dinner for the Gorbachevs: Front-Row Seat on World History." *New York Times,* December 9, 1987.

———. "Washington Talk: The White House; Why a Football Coach Dines with Mme. Chirac." *New York Times,* June 9, 1987.

———. "A White House Dinner for Jordan's King and Queen." *New York Times,* November 3, 1981.

———. "The White House: Keeping House to the Tune of $4 Million a Year." *New York Times,* October 29, 1982.

Gerstenzang, James. "Insider Of Oysters, Veal and Other Delicate Affairs of State." *Los Angeles Times,* July 24, 1990.

Getlin, Josh. "Reagan Stirs Tempest in a Bottle." *Los Angeles Times,* September 20, 1985.

Hughes Crowley, Carolyn. "Hail to the Chef at White House State Dinners." *Los Angeles Times,* July 24, 1986.

Hunter, Marjorie. "The Stately Home that is the White House." *New York Times,* January 18, 1981.

Johnson, Haynes. *The Working White House.* New York: Praeger Publishers, 1975.

Kaytor, Marilyn. "Upstairs in the Family Dining Room, Private Parties are Formal Yet Relaxed." *New York Times,* October 25, 1981.

Kirk, Elise K. *Music at the White House: A History of the American Spirit.* Urbana and Chicago, Ill.: University of Illinois Press, 1986.

Klapthor, Margaret Brown. *The Dresses of the First Ladies of the White House.* Washington, D.C.: Smithsonian Institution, 1952.

———. *Official White House China, 1789 to the Present.* Washington, D.C.: Smithsonian Institution Press, 1975.

Krebs, Albin and Robert Thomas Jr. "Nancy Reagan Wins Support on China Issue." *New York Times,* October 16, 1981.

Lauter, David. "Gorbachevs Try Bush Hospitality, Skip Wine." *Los Angeles Times,* June 1, 1990.

Manis, Andrew Michael. *Macon Black and White: An Unutterable Separation in the American Century.* Macon, Ga.: Mercer University Press, 2004.

Marshall, John. *The Life of George Washington: Commander in Chief of the American Forces.* Philadelphia: J. Crissy, 1832.

Martin, Judith. "Miss Manners." *Washington Post*, November 6, 1988.

McCullough, David. *John Adams*. New York: Simon & Schuster, 2001.

Menendez, Albert J. *Christmas in the White House*. Philadelphia: The Westminster Press, 1983.

Monkman, Betty C. *The White House: Its Historic Furnishings and First Families*. Washington, D.C.: Abbeville Press and the White House Historical Association, 2000.

Nemy, Enid. "Word from Friends: A New White House Style is on the Way." *New York Times*, November 9, 1980.

Nevins, Allan. *Grover Cleveland: A Study in Courage*. New York: Dodd, Mead & Co., 1948.

"Pale but Kicking Up Her Heels, First Lady's Happy to Be Home." *Los Angeles Times*, October 22, 1987.

Radcliffe, Donnie and Elizabeth Kastor. "The Night of the Peacemakers." *Washington Post*, December 9, 1987.

"Reagan Bids Adieu to Mrs. Thatcher." *New York Times*, November 17, 1988.

Reagan, Nancy, with William Novak. *My Turn: The Memoirs of Nancy Reagan*. New York: Random House, 1989.

Reynolds, Nancy. "In Defense of Mrs. Reagan." *New York Times*, March 5, 1987.

Roosevelt, Selwa. *Keeper of the Gate*. New York: Simon & Schuster, 1990.

Rosellini, Lynn. "A Christmas Potpourri, White House Style." *New York Times*, December 23, 1981.

———. "Concocting a State Dinner Guest List." *New York Times*, November 2, 1981.

Schafer, Susanne M. "Mrs. Reagan: 'It's Not Been a Great Year.'" *Los Angeles Times*, December 18, 1987.

Schifando, Peter, and Jean H. Mathison. *Class Act: William Haines, Legendary Hollywood Decorator*. New York: Pointed Leaf Press, 2005.

Seale, William. *The President's House, Volumes I & II*. Washington, D.C.: White House Historical Association with the cooperation of the National Geographic Society, 1986.

———. *The White House: The History of an American Idea*. Washington, D.C.: The American Institute of Architects Press, in association with The White House Historical Association, 1992.

Seale, William, et al., eds. *The White House: Actors and Observers*. Boston: Northeastern University Press, 2002.

"Sentimental Last Tour: Teary-Eyed Nancy Shows White House Decorations." *Los Angeles Times*, December 12, 1988.

Shultz, George P. *Turmoil and Triumph: My Years as Secretary of State*. New York: Scribner's, 1993.

Singleton, Esther. *The Story of the White House*. New York: The McClure Co., 1907.

Smith, Margaret Bayard. *The First Forty Years of Washington Society*. New York: Charles Scribner's Sons, 1906.

Smith, Marie. *Entertaining in the White House*. Washington, D.C.: Acropolis Books, 1967.

Spillman, Jane Shadel. *White House Glassware: Two Centuries of Presidential Entertaining*. Washington, D.C.: White House Historical Association, 1989.

Stein, Jeannine. "Inside Nancy Reagan's White House." *Los Angeles Times*, March 3, 1989.

Temple, Dottie, and Stan Finegold. *Flowers, White House Style*. New York: Simon & Schuster, 2002.

West, J. B., with Mary Lynn Kotz. *Upstairs at the White House*. New York: Coward, McCann & Geoghegan, Inc., 1973.

Whitcomb, John, and Claire Whitcomb. *Real Life at the White House*. New York: Routledge, 2000.

The White House: An Historic Guide. 15th ed. Washington, D.C.: White House Historical Association, 1982.

Willets, Gilson. *Inside History of the White House*. New York: The Christian Herald, 1908.

Williams, Marjorie, and Sarah Booth Conroy. "Guess Who's Coming . . . The Ins and Outs of Joining the Gorbachevs at the White House State Dinner." *Washington Post*, December 8, 1987.

Yoffe, Emily. "Pomp and Petits Fours with Ron and Nancy." *Wall Street Journal*, March 8, 1984.

IMAGE CREDITS